I0062987

SHE GROWS

RICH

HOW TO BECOME A
FINANCIAL POWERHOUSE

AUDREY FAUST

She Grows Rich
Copyright © 2025 Thought Leader Academy Publishing

All rights reserved. No part of this publication may be reproduced, distributed, or transmitted in any form or by any electronic or mechanical means, including photocopying, recording, or information storage and retrieval systems, without prior written permission in writing of Thought Leader Academy Publishing, or its duly authorized agent, except in the case of brief quotations embodied in reviews and certain other non-commercial uses permitted by copyright law. For information regarding permission, contact the publisher.

Cover design by Claudine Mansour Design. Interior design by Michael Beas.
Interior Image Design by Maria Conigliraro of Inspired Studios.

Disclaimer: The following is for informational purposes only and should not be considered as financial advice. Always consult with a financial advisor before making any investment decisions. Some names and distinguishing characteristics of individuals and organizations represented in this book have been changed to respect confidentiality. While best efforts have been made in preparing this book, the author and publisher make no warranty, representation, or guarantee with respect to the accuracy or completeness of information contained herein.

Published by Thought Leader Academy Publishing
3901 North Kildare Ave
Chicago, IL | 60641

Paperback ISBN: 979-8-9922572-0-5

Dedication

To all the women who believe they cannot become financial powerhouses – yes, you can, and I'll show you how!

To Tony Robbins – your tapes have been a source of courage and inspiration over the decades, encouraging me to take action, level up, and invest in my personal development.

"Money is only a tool. It will take you wherever you wish, but it will not replace you as the driver."

– Ayn Rand

TABLE OF CONTENTS

Acknowledgements

Tremendous thanks to Sara Connell and her Thought Leader Academy – without your expertise, this book would have never been born. To my patient and kind editor, Mary Nelligan, and the creative design genius of Maria Conigliaro of Inspired Studios for the beautiful images in this book. To my close friend Susan Gatti, who inspired me to share my story. To my biz besties, Maria and Louise, who cheered me on every day. To my family and the loves of my life, Andy, Jared, Eric, and Leanne.

Description

Are you ready to become a Financial Powerhouse?

"She Grows Rich" details simple, achievable, step-by-step strategies to financial prosperity, creating confidence and empowerment around your personal finances.

- Women in the United States could not have a credit card in their own name until 1974.
- Women in the United States could not obtain a business loan without a male co-signer until 1988.

Whatever is holding you back from creating money, wealth, and prosperity, this book will help you overcome it. Whether it's mindset, knowledge, or fear, this book shows you a clear path in a very simple way to start building your wealth and create financial independence for yourself and future generations. When we become financially empowered, it creates a ripple effect.

"She Grows Rich" will show you how to overcome any mindset blocks and provide a step-by-step plan to start investing.

In this book, Audrey Faust – a woman, mother of three, grandmother of two, business owner, and coach – shares exactly how she grew her wealth from nothing to becoming a multi-millionaire. She also shares stories of other women she's helped start growing their wealth and how simple it can be.

Inside, you'll learn:

- How to identify and remove money mindset blocks
- How to create a positive and powerful relationship with money
- How to develop a prosperity blueprint that supports you without feeling constrained
- Understanding your money personality and using it to empower you

- Recognizing and preventing emotional buying
- How to track and grow your net worth
- The 7% rule for financing
- A simple, easy guide to investing in mutual funds

It's time for women to become financial powerhouses, build financial independence, and show future generations how it's done. Stand on your own financially and become a role model for financial empowerment.

MONEY
FLOWS EASILY
AND EFFORTLESSLY
INTO MY LIFE.

CHAPTER 1

DEAR POWERHOUSE

Dear Powerhouse,

Yes, you! A financial powerhouse. You are in exactly the right place at exactly the right time to achieve every dream you've ever had of wealth, prosperity, and financial abundance.

How can I know this? Because I have walked the path from lack to abundance and have built a career empowering other women to do the same.

My story begins in 1997 with my husband and I living on a joint income of only $24,000 a year and taking care of our two young children. I was 27 years old. It was the first year I did my own taxes. I took a class to learn how to do taxes and got a job at a tax office in our local mall. I thought this would be a good way to learn and make a little extra money during the evenings because we couldn't afford daycare for our two children, which is what I could make working full-time during the day.

I remember the day I actually did our joint tax return as if it were yesterday. It was a typical busy Saturday afternoon at our local mall. The normal hustle and bustle filled the air. People were seeking refuge from the cold winter outside by shopping and enjoying the warmth indoors. Our office was situated across from Auntie Anne's pretzel shop, and the inviting smell of fresh, warm pretzels was always in the air. But on this day, the familiar sweet scent did nothing to lighten the moment.

I diligently put our information into the computer program. After I finished and clicked the calculate button, I was immediately confused. The tax refund number on the screen was far bigger than I had expected. Why were we getting such a big refund?

At first, I was happy. Then I thought maybe I'd made a mistake and rechecked my work. That's when I realized we were getting the Earned Income Tax Credit. This is a kind of financial help that the government gives to people who are nearly at the poverty line. Though we didn't have much, I hadn't thought of us being nearly at the poverty line before. Seeing it there on the screen really made our situation sink in. Knowing we needed this help made me feel embarrassed and ashamed. I thought, "Am I really that poor that the government has to give me extra money?"

The thought of needing this credit upset me. It felt like I was being told I wasn't doing well enough, that I was so poor that the government had to step in. It was a hard thing to hear. I quickly wiped away my tears, hoping no one would see.

I kept asking myself, "How did I end up here? How did life get so hard?" This was a really low point in my life, but one that made me want to try harder to make a better life for my family and myself.

I could hear my mother's words ringing in my head: "Always make sure you can support yourself." Growing up, she'd repeat this to me often. I didn't pay much attention then, but her words became important to me at that moment at the mall.

My mom hadn't shared these words to be mean or to frighten me. She said them because of her own life experiences. She had been trapped in a marriage she wasn't happy with, reliant on someone else for money, feeling like there was no way out. While my marriage was a happy one, I knew that I never wanted to be financially dependent on anyone else. I also knew that life could be unpredictable and things could change. I was raised to stand on my own two feet, but right then, I felt far from that.

She didn't want me to fall into the same situation she had experienced. Her words meant more than having money in my pocket. They were about resilience, facing life's challenges head-on, and ensuring that I could always meet my own needs.

At this moment in my life, I knew something had to change. I had to try harder and do better, not only for me but for my kids, too. They deserved a world full of choices, not limitations. I vowed to change my path. I began to see my financial struggles not as a sign of failure but as stepping stones to help me become the person my mom knew I could be.

Yes, it felt tough and scary, but it also marked the start of an exciting new chapter in my life.

I found myself at a crossroads and was unsure what to do. Fueled by a strong need to change, I found the courage to make a bold decision: I would go to college as an adult to study accounting.

This choice sparked fear upon fear within me. Growing up, my brother often belittled my intelligence, frequently calling me stupid. I had no other choice but to believe him at the time. I was three years younger and looked up to him. To me, everything he said was the truth. He was unknowingly programming my subconscious to believe his opinion of me. If he said I was stupid, then I must be. I think this is why I struggled so much in school as a child. His hurtful words made me doubt my ability to go to college after high school. Because of my constant doubt in my ability, I was so scared I didn't even take the SATs. My struggles in school made me feel like I wasn't meant for success.

But even with these old doubts, I knew I needed to change. I found inspiration from listening to Tony Robbins' motivational tapes and decided to face my fears and try higher education. I actually did well in my high school accounting class, and I clung to this tiny scrap of confidence as I began to consider college. Even though I knew the journey would be tough, I knew that getting a degree was important to becoming independent and building a better future for myself. I was ready to tackle whatever came my way.

Back then, going to college seemed like the only way out of my situation. Now, 20 years later, as a successful business owner and business financial coach for women, I know there are many ways to achieve success, and college is only one of those many options. But during those difficult times, getting a degree seemed like the only way toward a better future.

When I took that first college-level accounting class, owning a business that helped other women sort out their finances wasn't even a flicker in my mind. It's funny how life works out, sometimes leading us down paths we never thought possible. The universe often has bigger plans for us than we can even imagine. But the idea of going back to school, getting a degree, and learning new things—that felt real, and even though it was scary, it seemed possible because it was the only idea I had to help myself out of our financial situation. I had no idea how much this choice would change my life and make me feel powerful.

In the following years, I did better in college than I ever thought I could. It took me many years to earn my degree, much longer than if I had gone right after high school. I had taken a slower path, earning money at different jobs while studying and raising my children.

One of the jobs I worked through college was in the client service division at Vanguard, an investment company. The things I learned there, working part-time in the evenings, were amazingly valuable. I began to understand the stock market. I also learned about mutual funds and the power of investing. I worked there for a little over two years. I left when my kids started elementary school. I wanted to focus on finally finishing my accounting degree. I had enough courses under my belt to start my own bookkeeping business, so that's what I did. This allowed me to keep going to school and continue earning money for my family. We also added another little bundle of joy, a daughter, to our family, and that made five of us. Having my own business, which allowed me to work around the little one's schedules and continue school, was the perfect setup.

In 2008, after getting my bachelor's degree in accounting, I was full of pride and confidence. Before college, I wasn't sure if I could do well. But I didn't just do well - I did great! I finished college with a 3.8 GPA. This was a huge moment for me. It wasn't only about good grades; it was also about learning that I could do anything if I worked hard.

This success changed how I thought about myself. I felt smart, strong, and ready for anything. Feeling bold and excited, I decided it was time to grow my bookkeeping business. I wanted to take on bigger clients and have a bigger impact. I wanted to help them understand their business and how to make it grow. This was a fun new journey for me. And my success in college showed me that if you work hard enough, nothing is too far to reach.

Four years had passed since I graduated, and my children had begun to become more independent. One of my clients made an intriguing proposition, an opportunity I found impossible to turn down. My client wanted me to assume the role of Controller/CFO in his company, which would allow me to establish, nurture, and lead an entire accounting team. I found the prospect thrilling. Embracing this opportunity led to an exciting journey where we grew his business to new heights, and I grew and developed my leadership skills.

During this period, I was inspired to continue my education again, pursuing my MBA. This new chapter, ignited by another round of motivational tapes from Tony Robbins, brought up familiar fears. Yet, once again, I chose to face them, striving to broaden my knowledge.

In the following years, changes in the business resulted in a lengthy commute that left me feeling restless. Yearning for the excitement of a fresh endeavor and the autonomy my own business could provide, I returned to my entrepreneurial roots. This time, my goal was not only to offer accounting services but to empower other business owners. Drawing on my experiences as the CFO/Controller, where we increased the company's revenue from less than $1 million to over $5 million within a decade, I wanted to guide business owners in harnessing the power of their financial data to facilitate their businesses' expansion.

The wealth of knowledge and expertise I had attained while aiding in the growth of that small business was invaluable, an asset I was now eager to share with other ambitious business owners. Let me reiterate: knowledge is wealth! Little did I know that this would lead to the multi-six-figure CFO and Business Financial Coaching business that I love and cherish today.

I AM WORTHY OF

ABUNDANCE

AND FINANCIAL

PROSPERITY.

In the years that followed, I surprised even myself by transforming my financial narrative again. I had come so far from a joint income of only $24,000 per year, but I still had new heights to reach.

During a vacation to the Dominican Republic with dear friends, one of my closest friends, Susan, posed a question that got me thinking. We were sitting around the hotel pool sipping cocktails when she looked at me over her signature oversized sunglasses and said, "Why aren't you sharing your story of how you have created this incredible life?"

At first, I didn't get what she meant. I thought, *who would care about my story?* And to be honest, sharing my life story felt a little frightening. Would people think I was showing off?

Would they think differently about me? But the more I thought about it, the more I realized that Susan had a point. By telling my story, I could inspire other women. I could help them see what they could do and guide them in building their own wealth. Wouldn't that be a totally amazing thing to share?

Not long after this important chat with Susan, a colleague, Leilani, who I really admired, gave me a surprise compliment. "You're a real whiz at building wealth and smart about money matters. I would love to learn from you," she said. Hearing that from her, someone I looked up to, felt like she was inviting me to sit on a special throne that I didn't even know was meant for me. Sure, I knew a lot about money and how to grow wealth, but Leilani's words made me feel like I was a queen of it all. Her compliment felt like a sign from the universe, echoing what Susan had said and validating my next steps. Being a financially minded person and driven by curiosity, I decided to track and assess my progress in growing my wealth on a graph. I am a visual person, so I wanted to see exactly what I had accomplished.

NET WORTH

551% GROWTH
OVER A 15-YEAR PERIOD

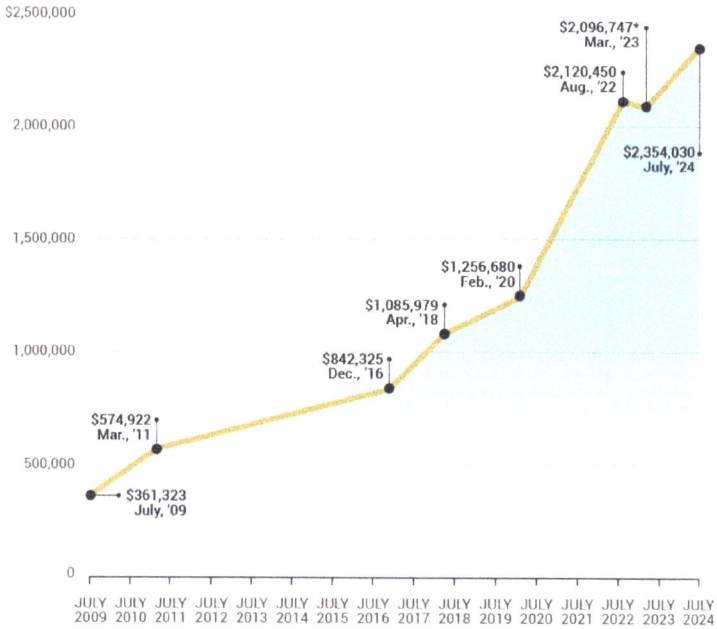

$2,096,747*
Mar., '23

$2,120,450
Aug., '22

$2,354,030
July, '24

$1,256,680
Feb., '20

$1,085,979
Apr., '18

$842,325
Dec., '16

$574,922
Mar., '11

$361,323
July, '09

$2,500,000	
2,000,000	
1,500,000	
1,000,000	
500,000	
0	

JULY 2009 · JULY 2010 · JULY 2011 · JULY 2012 · JULY 2013 · JULY 2014 · JULY 2015 · JULY 2016 · JULY 2017 · JULY 2018 · JULY 2019 · JULY 2020 · JULY 2021 · JULY 2022 · JULY 2023 · JULY 2024

*Net worth went down due to Stock Market drop and selling of 2 properties to buy one

8

Starting from 2009, a year after I graduated from college, I meticulously calculated my net worth and plotted it on a graph. As I witnessed the transformation unfold—from $350,000 in 2009 to over $2 million today, a 500% increase—I realized that I had a responsibility to share my story. I wanted to help more women achieve the same level of financial success and abundance that I had attained.

As my passion for sharing my story with others grew, I discovered a startling statistic: only 8.8% of US adults have a net worth of $1,000,000 or more, and a mere 33% of that group are women. This realization was shocking, and it underscored the need for more resources and guidance for women who seek financial success.

Unfortunately, many women don't have access to sufficient resources and lack the knowledge and skills needed to achieve financial independence. As a result, they may struggle to build the wealth they need to support themselves and their families. It's a problem that affects many women and one that I'm passionate about addressing and solving.

My passion for empowering women led me to organize the Financially Empowered Sisterhood (FES), a community where women supported each other as they learned and grew their financial knowledge. Although I am no longer running the FES group, the principles and strategies we explored together live on in the pages of this book. I am now fully focused on acting as a financial business coach for women.

In FES, we explored everything I will be sharing with you in She Grows Rich. I showed them the path to prosperity, the same path that leads to growing rich, as outlined in each chapter of this book. Every chapter in She Grows Rich corresponds to a week of the group program where I personally guided women in this group through each step on the path to prosperity, the very path that leads to growing rich. They learned, shared their struggles, and celebrated their wins all together in this amazing community.

In the following pages, I'm inviting you to come along on an amazing journey and follow this path. You will learn everything I teach the women in FES, as well as be guided through powerful mantras and journal prompts. It's about self-discovery, learning how to master your finances, and exploring all the exciting possibilities your future can hold. We'll dive deep into the key principles, the helpful strategies, and the important changes in mindset that have pushed me and other women forward. They've helped me and others face and overcome challenges and build a life full of incredible wealth.

You will hear a lot of my story, as well as stories from my clients and women in the FES group. You'll see how they used these same strategies to make significant changes in their own lives. Best of all, you'll learn how to apply these strategies to your own life.

Turning the pages of this book doesn't come with grand promises of instant riches. Instead, I'll share insights into recognizing beliefs and behaviors that might be slowing you down and how to chart a course toward your goals. Whether your goal is $100K in savings or reaching a $1M net worth, the journey is yours to claim.

Building wealth isn't a sprint; it's a marathon. Challenges will pop up, but with the right knowledge and mindset from this book, you'll be equipped to face them and keep growing your wealth. You'll be able to overcome any financial situation and keep moving forward with financial empowerment to build your path to prosperity. We'll talk about building your dream life and will back it up with a financial plan to get you there. As long as you're willing to get in and stay in the game of building wealth, I'll show you how slow and steady wins the race.

This book is specifically tailored for women who aspire to grow their wealth and gain the confidence and peace of mind that comes with knowing they are forging ahead on a path to prosperity. Every chapter equips you with actionable steps, unique insights, and practical bite-size strategies that you can implement immediately. Regardless of whether you are embarking on a new financial journey or seeking to elevate your existing wealth, I am sure you will elevate your financial know-how. Together, let us dive into growing your wealth, nurturing your financial independence, and becoming a financially empowered powerhouse. You'll gain the confidence that you are on a path to prosperity to build a secure future for yourself and your loved ones. You are a powerhouse. It is what you deserve.

Prompt: To know where you're going, know where you've been. How do you feel about your current financial well-being?

_____

_____

_____

_____

_____

_____

_____

_____

_____

_____

_____

_____

_____

_____

_____

_____

_____

Now, set the stage for success: What financial realities would feel freeing, amazing, and empowering? They're right there in front of you. Reach out and grab them!

_____

_____

_____

_____

_____

_____

_____

_____

_____

_____

_____

_____

_____

_____

I ATTRACT MONEY AND
OPPORTUNITIES THAT
ALIGN WITH MY VALUES
AND GOALS.

CHAPTER 2

WHAT YOU FOCUS ON GROWS

I magine the excitement of achieving a major milestone. Check back in with the last chapter's prompt and really tap into the energy of having that special thing or hitting that particular goal. For me, one of those goals was purchasing a second home in the picturesque paradise of Naples, Florida. When I finally achieved it, I was bursting with joy. I shared this accomplishment on social media, and what happened next caught me off guard —a comment from a friend of a friend asking, "What does your husband do that you can afford such a luxurious investment?" This remark triggered a fire within me. How was it that this outdated belief that men are always the primary financial provider in the household still exists in our society today?

This was a pivotal moment in my life. As the comment stared back at me from the screen, I couldn't help but feel frustration and also sadness. It was as if I was transported back to an era where a woman's financial accomplishments were attributed solely to her husband. Little did this commenter know that I was actually the financial wizard of our family, the driving force behind our wealth-building endeavors, not my husband.

While reflecting on this and our wealth-building journey, a funny memory emerged. In the early days of our relationship, my husband's bank account statement arrived in the mail. I offered to balance his checkbook, only to discover that his register was completely blank. Perplexed, I asked, "Where do you keep track of the checks you've written?"

He responded with a smile, "I don't. The bank calls me when I need to transfer money." It was then that I realized I would be the one taking care of our family's financial affairs from now on.

Fast-forward to today. I have a supportive husband who proudly shares with his friends and family how I am the backbone of our financial stability. This brings me immense joy and happiness. However, the comment on Facebook reminded me that outdated mindsets still exist in our modern society. The notion that it must be the man who holds the financial reins persists, perpetuating an unfair bias against women. Yet, we women are the pioneers, the trailblazers of our generation, breaking barriers and shattering these stereotypes.

Did you know that women weren't even allowed to have their own credit cards until 1974? I was stunned when I learned this. It shed light on my mother's struggles and the choices she felt trapped her in an unhappy, unstable marriage. She didn't have the freedom or options that we enjoy today. It became clear why my mother emphasized to me the importance of being financially independent and never relying solely on a partner for support.

A friend and colleague of mine, Maggie, runs a podcast with her mother called "Women & Money - The Shit We don't talk about. She is such a brilliant resource for women looking to become financially savvy, and she and I are aligned in our mission on financial empowerment.

She once told me, "A man is not a financial plan." I want to say it again: A man, or any partner for that matter, is *not* a financial plan. As painful as it can be to think about, that person you're relying on for financial stability may not always be around for one reason or another. As women, we need to make sure we understand and are empowered around our own finances because, historically, this information has been kept from us.

It is essential to recognize a significant fact: while 80% of men die married, i.e., before their spouses, approximately 80% of women will die single due to either their spouse dying before them or being unmarried. This means that at some point in our lives as women, we will need to understand, manage, and grow wealth on our own. Of course, this also includes the important work of estate planning. Financial education is critically important for women, as it becomes even more crucial to have the knowledge and skills to navigate their financial journeys independently as they age.

In fact, in a recent study by McKinsey & Company, women are the next wave of growth in the US wealth management industry. By 2030, women will be controlling as much as $30 trillion in financial assets. This is in part due to the fact that women, on average, marry older men, and on average, women outlive their partners by five years. So, as women, it is essential to financially educate ourselves because the facts are, even if we're not already, we will be managing the household finances ourselves at some point in our lives. We should be educating and empowering ourselves to assume this responsibility.

Additionally, in a recent survey conducted by Fidelity Investments asking women their two biggest regrets, 32% of women over 36 said their biggest financial regret was waiting too long to start investing for retirement. The reason they waited was because they didn't have the confidence to take the first step. Also, in this study, a whopping 71% of women over 36 said their biggest regret was not having a financial plan or budget because this is a vital piece of the puzzle for anyone trying to improve their financial situation.

My hope for you is that after reading this book, you will not be one of those women with either of these regrets. Soon, we'll get to the chapters that show you how to create a financial plan, get started in investing in your retirement, and so much more so you feel empowered and educated in building your path to prosperity.

Women often don't feel confident and empowered when it comes to managing their money. Another study by Fidelity (I like studies and numbers, what can I say!) showed that 92% of women want to learn more about financial planning and retirement. But, only 47% of them feel confident talking about money and investments with a financial professional.

The reasons behind this lack of confidence can be attributed to various factors.

Traditionally, women have been discouraged or excluded from discussions about money and investing. Society's gender norms have perpetuated the notion that financial matters are more suited to men, leaving many women feeling unprepared or inadequate in this domain.

Additionally, the financial industry has not always been inclusive or tailored to the unique needs and perspectives of women. The lack of relatable role models and accessible financial education has further contributed to the existing disparity in financial confidence between genders. My mission is to help bridge this gap and empower women to feel more confident in managing their finances personally and in their businesses.

I AM A MAGNET

FOR FINANCIAL SUCCESS AND PROSPERITY.

Let's talk about women in business for a minute. In the past, the entrepreneurial landscape was predominantly male-dominated, with less than 5% of business owners being women in the 1970s. However, the tide has shifted significantly. Today, an impressive 42% of business owners are women, a remarkable 740% increase. Wow! These figures underscore the exceptional leadership qualities and capabilities of women. Let me be clear: You are capable of this! Whether you're already a business owner or it hasn't ever crossed your mind to be one, you are smart enough and resourceful enough to be the one who runs this show.

As eager as I am to celebrate the successes of women in business, I also want to acknowledge that challenges persist. A recent survey by the National Women's Business Council revealed that only 40% of women business owners felt confident in their financial knowledge.

This signifies that 60% of women owners would benefit from support and guidance to gain greater confidence in managing their finances.

As an entrepreneur and business owner myself, I can attest that understanding and managing your finances is essential for success. In fact, studies have shown that regularly reviewing and analyzing your finances can significantly increase your chances of success. According to research from the Small Business Development Council, business owners who actively monitor their financials on a monthly basis are 80% more likely to achieve long-term success.

Why is this the case? When you regularly examine your financial statements, such as your income statement, balance sheet, and cash flow statement, you gain crucial insights into the financial health of your business. In the same way, when we regularly examine our personal finances by creating a financial plan and tracking our net worth, we are more likely to achieve greater wealth. Tracking your finances enables you to make informed decisions, identify areas for improvement, and seize opportunities for growth. And as I always say, "What You Focus on Grows."

"What You Focus on Grows" is a mantra that underscores the importance of attention and intentionality. When you consistently prioritize your finances and devote time to understanding and improving them, you create a foundation for growth. It's not about passive monitoring; it's about actively seeking opportunities to optimize and capitalize on your financial resources.

Remember, your finances are a powerful tool for strategic decision-making. By embracing a proactive mindset and dedicating regular time to review and analyze your finances, you position yourself for success. With every focused effort you put into understanding and improving your financial health, you pave the way for you to thrive and reach new heights.

And you're already beginning that effort! This book is evidence of that focus. The principles and strategies in the upcoming chapters will greatly increase your financial knowledge, help you achieve financial independence, and create a path to prosperity.

Empowering and educating ourselves not only benefits us personally but also has a profound impact on future generations, especially our daughters. By becoming financially educated and independent, we set a powerful example for the younger female generation, showing them the importance of financial literacy and the value of being in control of their own financial destiny.

By giving back in this way, we contribute to a future where women are not limited or constrained by financial barriers. We cultivate a culture where women are encouraged and supported in their pursuit of financial independence. Through our actions and teachings, we create a legacy of empowerment and inspire generations to come.

We are promoting financial literacy among women and breaking down any gender barriers as we challenge the status quo and redefine societal expectations. We envision a future where women are not only equal but excel in financial knowledge, taking on leadership roles in managing their personal and business finances and investments.

Imagine a world where all women break free from societal limitations AND courageously overcome obstacles to achieve their dreams. Picture a future where astonishing stories of success fuel our journeys, igniting a passion for change. Let us envision a world where women lead in bridging the gap in financial knowledge, creating a future where success knows no gender boundaries. This vision starts with you!

In this future, women are not viewed as secondary figures in financial matters but rather as indispensable contributors who bring diverse perspectives, innovative ideas, and a deep understanding of financial management to the table. Our goal is to challenge and dismantle the notion that financial acumen is solely the domain of men and to replace it with the expectation that women will not only be present but excel in this field.

By nurturing a generation of financially empowered women, we lay the foundation for this future. We foster an environment that supports and encourages women to pursue financial education, take control of their finances, and actively engage in financial decision-making processes. Through mentorship, education, and advocacy, we ensure that women are equipped with the skills and knowledge needed to thrive in the financial world.

Together, let us work towards a future where women's financial expertise is not only recognized but expected, where gender equality in financial matters becomes the norm, and where women's contributions to financial decision-making are celebrated. By breaking down barriers and championing financial education, we can pave the way for a future where women truly shine at the financial table.

In our pursuit of financial empowerment and equality, we strive to eradicate deeply ingrained stereotypes that limit and undermine women's achievements. Never again should a woman be asked, "What does your husband do for you to afford a second home in Florida?" We are determined to remove these stereotypes completely from our societal fabric.

Our financial success and accomplishments would never be attributed solely to the support or contributions of others. We are capable and deserving of building our own wealth, making our own financial decisions, and achieving our own dreams. It is time to challenge and dismantle the notion that a woman's financial achievements are contingent upon someone else's actions or capabilities. Let us build a society where women are not defined by the financial decisions or achievements of their partners but rather by their own hard work, determination, and financial acumen.

By continuing to read this book, you are embarking on a powerful journey of self-empowerment and transformation. The knowledge and insights shared within these pages will not only equip you with the tools to achieve your own financial independence but also enable you to inspire and empower future generations, including your daughters.

As you absorb the valuable information and strategies presented here, you are becoming part of a movement—a movement that seeks to break down barriers and empower women through financial literacy. By educating yourself and embracing financial independence, you are contributing to a larger cause, igniting a spark of change that ripples through your community and beyond.

As you continue on this journey, I encourage you to share your newfound knowledge and experiences with others. Engage in conversations about personal finance, uplift and support other women in their pursuit of financial literacy, and spread awareness about the importance of financial independence. Together, we can create a movement where women from all walks of life are empowered to take control of their finances and secure a brighter future for themselves and their families.

Remember, you are not alone on this path. This book serves as a guiding light, providing you with the knowledge, strategies, and inspiration you need to thrive financially. By arming yourself with financial literacy, you are building a solid foundation for yourself and future generations.

Let us continue reading, learning, and growing together. In the next chapter, we will start by creating a dream life and a vision to learn how to make your financial goals a reality. And together, we can create a powerful movement that starts with you and expands to financial literacy for all women—one that transcends barriers, empowers individuals, and transforms lives. Together, we can shape a future where women are financially empowered, equipped, and celebrated.

Prompt: Consider your "herstory." What role did your mother play in your family's financial life? What about your grandmothers, and their mothers, if you have this information? How do you feel considering the financial well-being of the women you came from?

_____

_____

_____

_____

_____

_____

_____

_____

_____

_____

_____

_____

_____

_____

_____

Now, consider yourself and future generations—your daughters, if you have children or any other young women in your life. How can you model financial wellness for them? How can you model it for yourself?

_____

_____

_____

_____

_____

_____

_____

_____

_____

_____

_____

_____

_____

_____

_____

_____

_____

_____

I AM GRATEFUL

FOR THE MONEY I HAVE

AND THE

ABUNDANCE

THAT SURROUNDS ME.

CHAPTER 3

DREAM BIG:

YOUR BEST LIFE IS WAITING

In this chapter, let's dive into creating a path to prosperity for you by painting a picture of the life you've always wanted. Yes, you heard it right. Dream big! Bigger than you've ever dreamed before! I'm right here with you, cheering you on because, believe it or not, you can have it all. There is no dream too big, and every single one of them can come true!

You see, my professional life began in the world of accounting. I'm a practical thinker, and, for me, dreams had to have proof. If something didn't add up, I didn't think it could happen. If you find yourself nodding along, I get it. You're used to relying on logic and reason. You might believe a new house, a vacation home, or a rental property is out of reach or that they are only for the smartest, the most educated, or the wealthiest.

But I am here to fuel your hope. I want you to believe, genuinely believe, that every single one of us, yes, *everyone*, can make their dreams a reality. I've already told you that I wasn't born with a silver spoon in my mouth. My parents struggled day in and day out, always balancing their bills, always striving to make ends meet. We had a small house with one bathroom shared between the five of us, and while we had the basics, enough to eat and clothes on our backs, this was always a struggle. My parents did the best they could, and our simple life was a good one, but I dream of more than existence for myself and for you.

My mom used to often say, "Money doesn't grow on trees," or "We work hard for our money." That was the mindset I grew up with. I'll dive more into this 'money mindset' in the next chapter. For now, let's say my background was humble and simple.

My parents made the best of what they had, and for that, I am eternally thankful. But because of that, my journey of starting to grow my wealth didn't start until I was much older. I did not learn wealth-building skills from my family of origin. And, to be honest, I didn't even realize I was building wealth until I was 40, and I started tracking it. I was figuring things out as I went along, and with time, I got better at it. That's why when my dear friend Susan, who has been with me through this journey, suggested I share my knowledge on building wealth with others, I was taken aback. Me? Really?

I used to be the girl who felt too ashamed to admit when I couldn't afford to go out for drinks with friends in my late twenties and early thirties. Now, I am someone who has built wealth step by step. What I didn't realize was that I was leading the way for others, like Susan, who watched closely and followed my path. As she followed me on this journey of building wealth, she often said she wouldn't have started if I hadn't shown her the way. That always warms my heart.

First, let's forget any guilt or blame you might feel about what you've done or not done so far. It's not your fault, and you can start right from where you are. Perhaps no one showed you how to do this, no one demonstrated what wealth looks like, or no one educated you on the fundamentals of personal finance. Remember, as women, we weren't even allowed to have a credit card until 1974. It's hard to believe, right? We're the first generation of women who can even have this kind of control over our money. So, how could we know the best way to handle our money if we were never taught? Let's change that. Let's build a new world for the next generation of strong women creating wealth. Let's show our daughters and sisters that knowledge gives us power. The more we understand money—how to take care of it, how to grow it, and how to build wealth—the stronger we become as a collective. We're on our way to ruling the world, so we need to know how to manage our money and grow our wealth.

Now that we've left behind guilt and shame, it's time to dream big. I wasn't always a big dreamer. But facts, statistics, and proof opened my eyes. I remember when I was 24, married with a home but no children yet. I was waiting in line at the grocery store when I saw an article on the cover of Money Magazine. It said a couple had saved up what seemed like a small fortune of $100,000 by saving $100 each month for 20 years. I thought, "Wow, maybe I can do that." I bought the magazine right away and read the article. It was inspiring! The couple had invested in something called a mutual fund, putting in $100 each month. Over 20 years, their investment grew to $100,000.

At that time, our money situation was tough. I remember trying to make a budget after we got married. Even before we added any fun activities, we were already running in the negative. It upset me so much that I threw that budget away. But I wasn't going to give up. I thought, "What if I put $50 each month into this thing called a mutual fund? What would happen?" I didn't even know what a mutual fund was, but it didn't matter. If those people in the article could do it, I believed I could do it, too. All the facts were in that article, and I trusted them. I started putting $50 each month into a mutual fund. That was the first step I took to build my wealth. This is where my journey began—saving only $50 every month.

There was also a strong reason or a "why" behind my savings. We lived in a small, old house that always needed repairs. The house was 50 years old, and we called the plumber so much he was on speed dial. I didn't really like that house much. My husband had picked it out prior to us being married. Yes, it was charming, but the kitchen was tiny. It only had one bathroom, and our main bedroom was so small it could barely fit a queen bed. I wanted a better house, but I knew we would need more money to get one. By saving that $50 every month, I knew that one day, it would help us make a down payment on a new home. My goal wasn't $100,000—it was around $40,000. That was my dream—to buy a $200,000 house, almost twice as expensive as our current one, and it had to be new or nearly new. For me, back then, this was a big dream, and I was set on making it come true.

Making dreams come true requires action, even if those actions start off small. Like developing any skill, growing your wealth requires patience, practice, and dedication. In the upcoming sections, I'll be providing plenty of ways for you to keep building your financial resilience. But first, let's focus on identifying and building your dream. Ready?

Step 1: Dream Boldly

It all begins with a dream, so ask yourself: What do you truly desire? What feels like a really large dream for you? Remember, no dream is too big or too small.

I've had the privilege of witnessing some truly remarkable dreams from my clients. One of them shared her aspiration to own a condo in sunny Florida, hoping for more time soaking in the sun and building stronger bonds with her husband's family.

Another client's dream was centered around financial security. She yearned for a robust savings account that would give her peace of mind and stability. The idea of money safely tucked away in the bank, ready for any situation, gave her a sense of immense comfort.

One of my clients dreamed about giving her kitchen a makeover. She imagined a welcoming, functional space where she could whip up delicious meals and enjoy warm, enjoyable moments with family and friends.

For another client, her dream was about enabling her husband to retire. She wished to gift him the leisure of time, allowing him to explore life beyond the constraints of a regular job.

Whether your dream revolves around a beach condo, a healthy savings account, a kitchen remodel, or a retirement plan for your loved one, let your dream resonate with your deepest desires. Envision it with all your senses – the more vivid it is, the stronger it will be.

Step 2: Make Your Dream Tangible

With your dream now alive in your mind, the next step is crucial - etching it into existence by writing it down. It might seem straightforward but don't underestimate the power of this simple act. When you put your dream into words, you're not only recording it but making it more tangible and real. It's a commitment you're making to yourself, a pact between you and your dream.

A fascinating piece of research reveals that you can boost your chances of achieving your dream by 42% by writing it down. Incredible, isn't it? Writing down your dream transforms it from a fleeting thought into something concrete and achievable. It makes your dream visible and holds you accountable, serving as a constant reminder of your goal.

Once you finish this chapter, find a quiet corner and start to write down your dream. There's a journaling space to do so right at the end! Be specific and detailed; it could be as simple as "I want to save X amount of dollars in two years" or as bold as "I will buy a beachfront property within the next five years."

The act of writing not only solidifies your intentions but also sends a powerful message to the universe. It says that you're serious about this dream and that you're ready to pour your energy and time into making it come true. So go ahead, make your dream tangible, and commit to it - write it down.

Step 3: Dive Deep into Your "Why"

This third step is a heartfelt and important one: it's about exploring why your dream is so meaningful to you. This is not about surface-level reasons; it's about connecting with the emotions that this dream stirs within you. What does realizing this dream signify for you and your family? What role will it play in your life?

Let me share a few experiences from my coaching clients. They've allowed me to share some of their personal "whys" and the emotional drive behind their dreams.

One client, a dedicated mother, shared her desire to offer a better version of herself to her children. Achieving her financial goals wasn't about providing materially for her family. It was about showing her kids what's possible when you dream big and commit.

And then there's a client who told me her wealth-building journey was fueled by her wish to help others. She aspired to be in a position where she could financially assist her family members or employees if they ever needed support.

Another beautiful example was of a client who wanted to give back to the charities she passionately supported in her profession as an event planner. She believed that financial abundance would enable her to contribute more generously and make a larger impact.

These are real people with real dreams, like you. And their "whys" come from a deep, emotional place. It's about more than financial success; it's about the feelings that financial independence can bring - peace, security, confidence, and the ability to make a difference in the lives of those we care about.

When you're writing down your "why," I encourage you to dig deep. Don't just skim the surface. Let your emotions guide you. The more heartfelt your reasons, the stronger the emotional connection you'll have with your dream. And that connection can be a powerful motivator on your journey to make your dream a reality.

Step 4: Bring Your Dream to Life with Images

Take your dream to the next level by transforming it into images. Look for pictures that embody your dream on the internet and place them where you can see them daily. Our brains are wired to process visuals very well, and this trick can truly boost your motivation. Consider crafting a vision board, a canvas full of images that inspire you and represent your dream. Once I started doing this, it added a whole new dimension to my goal-setting process.

A few years ago, I stumbled upon the magic of visualizing my goals. It was during my training under the esteemed Jack Canfield that I discovered a missing link in my goal-achieving process: the power of visualization. At first, I must admit that Canfield's suggestion of creating a vision board seemed like nonsense to me. Could it be possible that merely sticking pictures in front of me would bring my dreams to life? I was skeptical, but I decided to give it a shot. To my astonishment, it worked wonders! It was as if I had stumbled upon a secret ingredient that turbocharged my goal achievement.

Let me share an unforgettable experience that solidified my belief in the vision board. In January 2020, I set my sights on buying a house in the heavenly destination of Naples, FL. The crystal-clear waters, powdery white sands, and lush green surroundings had enchanted my husband and me during our 25th wedding anniversary celebration. However, I faced a hurdle: A previous mortgage broker informed me that having more than four mortgages without a rental property business would be practically impossible due to strict banking guidelines.

Nevertheless, I dared to put this dream on my vision board and see what would unfold. Carefully selecting images from the internet, I pasted them onto my board, each one representing an aspect of my dream. There was a mesmerizing ocean view with palm trees swaying in the breeze, an image of a balcony (or lanai as they call it in Florida) overlooking a beautiful green landscape with water in the background, and even the words "good vibes" etched in white sand. One striking picture featured a large, inviting king bed with a white desk in the background, and to my surprise, I now own that same white desk.

With my dream vividly displayed before me each day, it remained constantly on my mind. A few weeks later, fueled by curiosity, I approached my local bank to explore strategies for gathering enough funds to make my dream a reality. Despite my business income not being stellar at the time, I was determined to find a clear path to achieve my goal. To my amazement, my banker introduced me to a brilliant idea: not only pulling equity from my primary residence but also from one of my rental properties to buy the new place in cash through refinancing. I had never considered this option before.

I was in awe. It was really happening! Only a few months after crafting my vision board, my dream was unfolding right before my eyes. In March 2020, I submitted an offer, and by May, I proudly became the owner of a condo in Naples, FL, purchased entirely in cash, thanks to the equity from my other properties. The speed at which my dream became a reality left me astounded, turning me into a true believer.

If you're contemplating skipping this crucial step, I urge you to give it a shot. You have nothing to lose and everything to gain, perhaps even faster than you ever imagined. I know it might seem far-fetched that something as simple as creating a visual representation of your dream could bring it to life, but I challenge you to give it a try. What do you have to lose? At worst, you'll have some fun imagining your dream, and at best, you could find yourself accelerating toward your goal faster than you ever thought possible.

**I AM OPEN
AND RECEPTIVE TO NEW
FINANCIAL
OPPORTUNITIES
AND IDEAS.**

I wasn't always a natural saver. Quite the opposite, in fact. My mother would say I had "money burning a hole in my pocket." My older brother, the careful one, was adept at saving while I reveled in the thrill of new purchases. Yet, everything changed when I had a bigger dream in mind.

A vivid memory from my past illustrates this shift. I had my heart set on a new 10-speed bike and didn't want to wait until Christmas. I began doing extra chores, stashing away every penny from birthdays or odd jobs. With each dollar saved, I moved closer to my dream, a thrill that overshadowed any impulsive buy.

The day I finally had enough saved was unforgettable. Choosing that beautiful blue 10-speed bike was an unmatched experience. The pride of achieving my goal, the memory of purposeful and diligent saving, remains vivid even today. Every ride on that bike was a sweet reminder of my accomplishment.

Often, we limit ourselves, believing we're incapable of saving money or achieving something significant. But, when we apply a bit of effort - identifying a goal, writing it down, understanding its 'why' and visualizing it - our perceived impossibilities become achievable.

A few years back, I trained as a certified NeuroCoach, diving into the brain science behind realizing our dreams and goals. This coaching process teaches techniques to rewire our brains for success. It involves taking action, documenting it, understanding the emotions behind it, and creating mental images.

Understanding how our brains work led me to some additional tricks I like to use for achieving my goals. The question I always keep within sight on my desk is, **"Does this decision support my vision?"** Every time I consider a purchase or a business move, I challenge myself with this question. It's simple yet incredibly powerful, helping me navigate past monetary concerns and focus on the decision's essence. I guide my coaching clients in the same manner, asking them, **"If money wasn't a factor, what decision would you make?"** We often get hung up on the financial aspect, stagnating our progress and potential. When we eliminate this concern, it often becomes apparent that the decision aligns perfectly with our vision, and the only barrier is self-doubt.

Another question I use to make important decisions is, **"Will this decision make my future self proud?"** When I look back, I relish the brave choices I made, regardless of how intimidating they appeared at the time. I seldom regret venturing beyond my comfort zone. More often than not, the result surpasses my expectations, reinforcing that today's audacious decisions pave the path for a rewarding and triumphant tomorrow.

Recently, my husband and I were reminiscing about the remarkable real estate choices we made, some of which felt unnervingly risky at the time. However, taking those leaps of faith proved to be incredibly worthwhile, often with outcomes better than we could have anticipated.

In 1995, when we were newly married and expecting our first child, we took a vacation to Myrtle Beach, South Carolina, and fell in love with the place. A spontaneous thought struck us, "Why not buy a home here and rent it out to vacationers?" Being naive and in our 20s, we stepped into a realtor's office to explore this whimsical notion. But when the realtor asked if we had a 20% down payment ready for the rental property, reality hit us hard. We were far from having that kind of money, but the dream remained alive.

Fast forward to 2010, during the housing market crash, the idea of buying property at Myrtle Beach resurfaced. With diligent research and number crunching, we visited Myrtle Beach, inspected three properties on a short sale, and finally found our home. Despite it not being rentable to vacationers due to HOA regulations, it could still be rented long-term with the option of becoming our retirement home.

Although the process may sound smooth now, I was fraught with nervousness at the time. Questions flooded my mind.

Who am I to buy a rental property?

What if it doesn't get rented?

What if it becomes a financial drain?

What if this turns out to be our worst decision?

It was undeniably terrifying, but we bravely ventured forth. We hired a rental company, and within three weeks, our property was rented, covering their fee, the mortgage payment, and all other expenses.

The house remained rented for the twelve years we owned it, sitting vacant for only two or three weeks in total. In 2022, we decided to sell it to buy a retirement home in Florida. We sold it for double our original investment, having only put down a 20% deposit while rent covered all expenses over the years. None of the fearful scenarios I had envisioned ever came true.

Frequently, we stunt our growth by letting fear overpower us with unnerving 'what-ifs' that never come true. These negative thoughts can inhibit us from seizing exceptional opportunities. We must realize that the potential for greatness often resides outside our comfort zones, and occasionally, we need to gather our courage and make that leap.

One of my favorite aspects of coaching is guiding clients through these fearful thoughts, leading them down the 'what if' rabbit hole. Most of the time, they come to understand that even in the worst-case scenario, they'll pull through fine. Often, the best possible outcome or even something beyond their wildest dreams occurs. In my experience, there's a reward for facing fear and embracing risks. Overcoming fear can be challenging, but with each step forward, no matter how small, you are rewarded. Can you recall a few instances when this has been true for you? These examples will help your brain contest fear-based thoughts and prove them wrong.

I encourage you to dream big and not let fear hinder you. With each action you take, you either succeed or learn, making life an exciting journey of exploration and growth. Remaining stagnant out of fear offers no fun, no adventure, no challenge. Instead, imagine, what if your dream did come true? What if you made it happen?

As I reflect on my life and my progress, not only financially but also in my personal and business development, I find myself in a place I couldn't have imagined five years ago. If someone had told me I'd be writing a book about my financial journey back then, I would have dismissed the idea outright. Yet, here I am, sharing my story because I am deeply committed to helping other women build their wealth. It feels like a true calling.

Renowned motivational speaker Tony Robbins once said, "We often overestimate what we can achieve in a month and underestimate what we can achieve in a decade." This quote rings true in so many aspects of our lives. We should never limit our dreams and ambitions to the constraints of our current situation or immediate future. Rather, we should think about what we can achieve in the long term, not letting fear and self-doubt hold us back.

Prompt: Work through the four steps outlined in the previous chapter!

Step 1: Dream Boldly

Let yourself truly dream big and discover what you most want. If money wasn't a factor, what decision would you make? What would you do/ be/ have? Once you've really let yourself feel into your future, move on to:

Step 2: Make Your Dream Tangible

Write it down! Right here, right now:

_____

_____

_____

_____

_____

_____

_____

_____

_____

Step 3: Dive Deep into Your "Why"

Why do you want these beautiful big dreams? How would having/ being/ doing your dream make you feel?

_____

_____

_____

_____

_____

_____

_____

_____

_____

_____

_____

_____

_____

_____

Step 4: Bring Your Dream to Life with Images

In a separate space, whether digital or physical, put together a vision board. Tap into the feeling of your dream and make it visual!

MAKING MONEY

IS SO EASY.

CHAPTER 4

THE POWER OF MINDSET

In my many years of working as a coach and consultant and participating in various coaching groups myself, I've observed a multitude of mindsets and attitudes toward money. Many people firmly believe that they have a healthy money mindset. Still, as I spend time with them, uncovering the layers of their thoughts and beliefs, it becomes clear that growth and improvement are always possible for everyone.

Indeed, self-improvement is a never-ending journey. I still regularly work on mastering my own money mindset. It's a continuous process, and it's entirely okay to lose your balance once in a while, too.

In fact, I recently faced a challenging situation myself. 2023 was the final year my husband would run his landscaping business. He had decided to retire, which meant I was to become the sole income earner in our family. The change was massive, and I found myself worrying about the implications. To make matters worse, that year, we had an unusually snowless winter, and the snow removal part of his business suffered. Zero earnings for those brutal winter months only added to my financial angst.

I could feel myself slipping into a *scarcity mindset*, letting fear and worry consume my thoughts. What is a scarcity mindset? It is the pervasive belief that there isn't enough to go around. It is the feeling of famine or, *"Will I have enough to survive?"* You can have a scarcity mindset about anything, about time, friendship, or love. And certainly about money. This time, instead of feeling empowered by money, I felt desperate for it. Although we were financially stable, this stress started to manifest in various aspects of my life. I found myself irritable and anxious in ways I hadn't been for years as the tension escalated and our income dwindled. I reached a point of panic where I was reaching out to people who owed us money, trying to bring something, anything, in. This kind of behavior was totally out of character for me and not what I teach, and yet I couldn't break out of it.

After three stressful months, I finally recognized the scarcity pattern I had fallen into. I reminded myself that everything was okay and decided to break free from my worries. I realized that my fears and stress were not only affecting me, but they were also negatively impacting my relationships with my loved ones. Deep down, I knew we were financially stable, but I had allowed my fears to take the driver's seat, as we all do from time to time.

From that moment, I decided to retake control and choose trust over fear. I let go and chose to believe that everything would turn out fine, even if it didn't align with my original master plan. I started using this daily mantra, "Money comes to me easily and freely from multiple sources on a continuous basis," and things started turning around. This experience was a valuable lesson, showing me that even those who have spent years cultivating a healthy money mindset can fall victim to the fear and scarcity that money often brings, but I also had my tools to rely on to change my mindset. Mantras are a good quick fix if you find yourself in a lack or scarcity mentality. Try it now. Say it out loud to yourself. See how it shifts how you feel.

MONEY COMES TO ME

EASILY AND FREELY

FROM MULTIPLE SOURCES

ON A CONTINUOUS BASIS.

Understanding your money mindset is a crucial aspect of your journey toward wealth. It acts as your financial compass, shaping your decisions and, therefore, your outcomes. If this mindset is misaligned with your financial goals, it can unintentionally impede your progress.

Recognizing and modifying your money mindset is, therefore, essential.

Consider the T-E-A-R model to better grasp how your mindset operates: Your Thoughts trigger Emotions, which create your Actions and ultimately lead to your Results. Almost all of your thoughts begin in your subconscious, which was greatly influenced before age seven. You literally have a seven-year-old running your brain until you make a conscious effort to change it. And, the seven-year-old only has exposure to whatever financial mindsets were prevalent in your family of origin. What did your parents believe about money? Your grandparents? For many of us, the people who raised us went through times of poverty and very likely responded by developing a scarcity mindset, and you very likely inherited it. This isn't to blame the people who came before you. They wanted to keep themselves safe and keep you safe, and unless they themselves did a lot of internal work, they probably didn't make clear, intentional choices in what money mindset they handed down to you.

The human brain is built for efficiency, defaulting to autopilot mode for routine activities. While this works well for tasks like tying shoes or riding a bike, it may pose challenges when it involves our thoughts about money. If you grew up in a household where money was scarce, where there was fighting around money or any type of difficult money challenges, you may have inadvertently cultivated some negative beliefs about it and not even known it. I like to call these negative thoughts and beliefs Prosperity Blockers.

T.E.A.R.

THOUGHT

CREATES AN

EMOTION

LEADS TO AN

ACTION

THAT CREATES YOUR

RESULTS

All these experiences, often unnoticed and often unremembered, shape your current money mindset. Reflect on your past for a moment. What kind of money narratives were you exposed to during your childhood? Do any specific scenes or words come to mind? The first crucial step towards fostering a healthier money mindset is identifying these Prosperity Blockers and understanding their influence on your life.

Fortunately, throughout my journey, I've developed effective strategies for recognizing and reshaping my clients' and my own money mindset, which I'm eager to share with you. Even if you believe your money mindset is already primed for prosperity, there's always room for growth and improvement. The exciting part about our malleable minds is that you can reprogram your subconscious, and I will show you how to begin this reprogramming with a simple exercise in this chapter. But the first step is to understand your existing money mindset. To do this, I'll pose five questions to you. While I often use some additional questions and more in-depth coaching techniques with my clients, these five questions will get you started.

This exercise will help you identify potential facets of your money mindset that may need adjusting. To begin, find a peaceful space, gather your thoughts, and make sure you have a pen. When you read the questions, you will write down the very first word that springs to mind without overthinking or doubting your immediate responses.

Your initial reactions are likely to provide a clear reflection of your subconscious mind, which commands a staggering 95% of your daily thoughts and, in turn, influences the majority of your decisions and actions. Remember to find yourself a quiet place, piece of paper and don't think; just write.

Here are the questions. Remember, write down the first word that comes to your mind. Don't overanalyze. If it doesn't make sense immediately, that's fine—we'll dissect it later. Allow yourself less than five seconds for each:

1. *Making money is* _____

2. *Rich people are* _____

3. *If I make more money, that means I am* _____

4. *Having a lot of money is* _____

5. *Saving money is* _____

Once you've noted down your responses, spend some time reflecting on them. How do they make you feel? Do they seem to be an accurate representation of your perceptions toward money? Did any of your answers surprise you or trigger an emotional response?

Next, try to evaluate the positive or negative tone of your responses. Your negative answers are your Prosperity Blockers. It's not uncommon to find at least two, and often four or five Prosperity Blockers. If that's the case for you, don't worry, I've got you. We'll walk through an exercise to remove these blockers before the end of this chapter. These Prosperity Blockers prevent you from accumulating wealth and abundance. This exercise gives you a glimpse of what's happening beneath your conscious awareness, offering a stepping stone towards positive change. The great news is that next, I'll be guiding you on how to rewire your brain to reshape your money mindset positively and eliminate your Prosperity Blockers for good.

Now, you may be unsure whether some of your answers are negative or positive. For instance, a response like "lucky" to questions 2-4 can swing either way. In my experience, however, this often leans toward the negative because it suggests that you believe wealth is attributed to luck, which you might feel you don't have or is outside of the scope of your control.

One popular response to the first question is "hard." For some reason, a lot of people believe that making money is hard or difficult. As I often work with entrepreneurs and small business owners, it's not surprising that this response is prevalent. I used to think the same way before I reworked my subconscious. As an entrepreneur, it can sometimes feel difficult to make money. There's no greater challenge than putting yourself out there, creating your own business, and searching for clients. Have you ever heard the phrase "pounding the pavement?" What a harsh way to describe building a business or making sales. It doesn't sound fun, does it?

Now that you've identified them, how can you remove your Prosperity Blockers? It's simpler than you may think, but it requires a little patience and time. I want to give you a straightforward, simple strategy you can start implementing today to remove your Prosperity Blockers. Are you ready to take the first step towards a transformative mindset shift? Let's do this together with my Prosperity Blocker Removal exercise.

Step One: Choose one negative response and find evidence of the contrary. If your subconscious thinks making money is hard, brainstorm instances where it was easy. It may take some time to recall a time when making money was effortless. You can also borrow evidence from others. Do you know someone who makes it seem easy? If so, think about them and use them as your example and proof that it is possible.

Presenting your brain with proof is a crucial step. Otherwise, it will doubt the reprogramming effort, rendering it ineffective. It might take you a few days to find evidence to the contrary, and that's completely okay. There's no rush. This belief has been with you for a long time, so taking a few more days to compile compelling stories that will convince your brain the belief is false isn't a big deal. As you find proof to the contrary of your Prosperity Blocker, write it here:

Step Two: Construct a fresh belief. For instance, if you're holding onto the idea that making money is hard or challenging, write down the opposite. Create your own personal Prosperity and Abundance Mantra by writing down the opposite: "Making money is easy." Now, recall the evidence you've found or the experiences you've had where making money felt easy, perhaps when you sold a few unwanted items online, sold a property or car, or earned doing something you loved and thought was fun. Even go back to your childhood if you can remember. Did you get an allowance? Did your parents give you money? Did you have a lemonade stand? How about gifts when you had a birthday or celebrated a holiday? Then, craft a sentence or two about these experiences, such as "Making money is easy when I sell things." Or even, "Making money is easy when I do this kind of work that I love." As a next step, don't only write down this new belief and evidence; engage with this new belief and involve your senses - read it out loud, visualize it, and feel the ease of making money. Aim to engage with this new belief at least three times a day. And write it here:

_____

_____

_____

_____

_____

_____

_____

Step Three – Commit to this new belief for a span of three months or longer. Write it, say it, visualize it, and feel it. Repeat the process three to four times daily. Why three months?

Scientific research indicates that while it takes approximately 21 days to develop a new habit and start observing results, it takes about 67 days to fully cement this new belief in your brain, thereby effectively creating a new neural pathway in your subconscious. This process of repetition and reinforcement will erase the old belief and supersede it with the new one, minimizing any chance of the old belief reappearing.

Removing Prosperity Blockers can lead to incredible transformations. This coaching exercise played a pivotal role in my client, Susan's, remarkable journey to mitigate fifteen straight months of losses in a new division of her six-figure consulting firm. Susan definitely had the drive and ambition to succeed. When we did the Prosperity Blocker Removal exercise together, Susan learned she had a Prosperity Blocker that making money is "hard." Together, we went deep into the roots of this belief, where it came from, and how it was influencing her decisions and actions in this new division. She was taking a lot of action, working a lot of hours, going on social media regularly, doing launch after launch, everything the experts told her to do, and yet still she'd had fifteen straight months of losses in this new division treading water at barely $5,000 per month in revenue.

Together, we worked through Steps One and Two, identifying times in her life when making money felt easy and using these times as opposite evidence to form her new belief. Susan committed to working on Step Three for the next couple of months on her own. The transformation was nothing short of awe-inspiring. Susan's business soared to new heights, and in three months' time, she had a remarkable $80,000 month, 16x her division's revenue. But what's even more remarkable is the lasting impact of the exercise. This division is now a profitable product in this leader's business.

Prosperity Blockers happen at every level of growth, and this exercise is what generated a profound impact and turned a financial challenge into a profitable division, almost overnight. I invite you to undertake this transformative journey yourself. By identifying and reshaping your Prosperity Blockers, you can tap into your immense potential and create a path to unparalleled success. Susan's transformation offers a glimmer of hope for anyone looking to break from limiting beliefs and achieve enduring prosperity. She learned that making money could be easy, and by finding the evidence and repeating the new belief over three months, she achieved a significant breakthrough.

And I know you can do it too. As stated in Step Two, your subconscious mind seeks repetition, but it also needs proof. Proof that the situation can change. Reflect on a time when something was easy for you, like a job or a business deal. In my case, I make money easily by renting out my properties. I simply earn by providing my home to others. Keep in mind that without proof that things can change, the process will stumble. Your brain needs assurance that change is feasible. The only way to convince it is by presenting evidence, so look for this proof everywhere.

Consider this example. Let's say you've always believed that "rich people are selfish." However, you recall a wealthy individual in your community who regularly donates to local charities, proving that not *all* rich individuals are selfish. In fact, these charities could not do the important work they do in the community without this benefactor. With this proof as evidence for your brain, you can construct a new belief: "Rich people are generous." For the next three months, write down this belief, read it aloud, visualize this generous person, and feel the positivity associated with wealth. Repeat this three to four times a day. By doing this consistently, you're not only creating a new belief but also reinforcing it in your subconscious, thereby permanently transforming your mindset around what it means to have wealth.

What I've noticed with coaching clients is that around the three-week mark, our brains start to resist the changes. You might experience a bit of a meltdown at this point. But if you do, know that this is a sign of progress. Keep going, allow the meltdown to happen, acknowledge it for what it is, and then let go of the thoughts. You can celebrate the fact that you are transforming your brain to create new neural pathways and shedding your Prosperity Blockers for good. Not everyone experiences this three-week meltdown, but if you do, you'll now know to expect it and be able to move past it and keep going.

RICH PEOPLE ARE KIND, GENEROUS, AND COMPASSIONATE.

Another way I was able to find evidence or proof was to take action and let my beliefs catch up. My husband talked with me about joining a country club. He was a big golfer, and so were our teenage children. I was not completely on board, but he convinced me that joining the country club would be beneficial for our kids' golfing skills. I always thought that country club people had lots of money, they were not *my people,* and I didn't belong there. But after about a year, we started meeting some fantastic people and became friends with them. And guess what? They were all normal and nice people, exactly like us. They weren't any different. In fact, they were friendlier than most people. This was an unexpected shift in my mindset that happened naturally. I had a preconceived notion that we weren't country club people because I had never experienced a country club before. This experience enabled me to find the evidence I needed to prove my belief was wrong.

And guess what happened? My husband gained clients for his business through the country club, which virtually covered the membership costs. Another unexpected bonus! All my preconceived notions about people who join country clubs were biases that I completely debunked. I started looking forward to going every week and catching up with our friends there. I'm not sure where that Prosperity Blocker originally came from. Our brains can often play tricks on us, nurturing Prosperity Blockers of which our conscious mind is unaware.

Let's talk about my client Kim as an example. Kim had started multiple businesses in the past, but surprisingly, she was worse off financially after each endeavor. Despite growing one venture to a seven-figure valuation, she still struggled to retain any of the money, let alone pay herself. We eventually discovered that a Prosperity Blocker had been ingrained in her since childhood. Kim's father, an entrepreneur himself, had a history of businesses failing and going bankrupt, leaving the family in increased debt. Observing this pattern during her formative years, Kim inadvertently internalized that owning a business equals strenuous work with little to no financial reward. Her Prosperity Blocker led her to spend her profits, prioritizing employee raises and unnecessary business expenses over her own financial well-being. Once we identified this hidden blocker, Kim felt a huge relief. She wasn't the cause of her business's failing; she was simply being guided by a Prosperity Blocker that unknowingly sabotaged her own success. Now, with this newfound awareness, Kim is working on my 3-step process to rewrite this belief and is increasing her profits while also rewarding herself.

Sometimes, the beliefs ingrained in us since childhood can be beneficial. My mom instilled in me a critical belief: as a woman, it's essential to be financially independent to avoid being stuck in an unwanted relationship. This fueled my own personal financial journey as well as my mission to help other women create this path. But not all of us are fortunate enough to have a parent who instilled in us useful financial information.

My understanding of the power of thought transformation came much later in life when I started working with a mindset coach in my late 40s. The realization that I had the power to control and change my thoughts was revolutionary for me. My time with a mindset coach, which lasted for around six months, was a turning point in my life. This was my first time investing in a coach, and the substantial fees were indeed a mindset shift in and of themselves. I was so nervous to invest in coaching. Would it really be worth it? I soon learned that the transformation is indeed in the transaction. The more you invest, the more committed you become, and the harder you work towards seeing results. And boy, did I work hard and see amazing results!

Let me illustrate this with an example. Suppose you bought a ticket to an event for $25, and something came up, and you couldn't make it. You might not fret over losing $25. But now, imagine you purchased a ticket to a gala event for $2,500 and faced the same issue. Would you miss the event? Chances are, you would go regardless, if at all possible. The same applies to hiring a coach. A $500 investment for a coach is going to feel different than if you invest $5,000 or even $15,000. At that higher price point, we make it a point to show up and do the work regardless of the circumstances. The more money we invest, the more committed we become to transformation.

Improving our mindset is a lifelong journey, whether it's related to money or our general outlook on life. It's an ongoing commitment that I've made to myself because we humans have a habit of getting tangled up in our narratives. It's the way we're wired. The more we flex and strengthen our mindset muscle, the richer our life experience becomes. We can truly savor the present and be free from the incessant chatter of our minds. Honestly, I believe that this is something we should be teaching in high school. I imagine how different it would be if I knew back then that I had the power to change my thoughts. That meditation could quiet the whirlwind of anxieties and hypothetical scenarios running through my mind. I can't even really imagine what my life would have looked like had I gotten this information sooner. I could've shared this empowering knowledge with my children at a young age and given them the tools to control their own thoughts. But all I can do is work to share this information now with them, with you, and with the clients I have the privilege to support.

If you're now only discovering the world of mindset development, you're not alone. As I mentioned earlier, I was in my late 40s when I stumbled upon it, and I'm still learning new things each day. Knowing there is the ability to change our subconscious minds with a simple formula is mind-blowing. One of the reasons I became a certified NeuroCoach is because if I could help people understand how to change their thoughts like my mindset coach did for me, I could help people change their money mindset and grow their wealth. I'm pleased to say that I've been successful in this work and have seen so many clients power through their Prosperity Blockers and achieve their financial dreams.

Prompt: Reflect on your Prosperity Blockers. Did any of them surprise you? How did the exercise make you feel? What did you learn from rewriting a blocker into a new, positive mindset?

_____

_____

_____

_____

_____

_____

_____

_____

_____

_____

_____

_____

_____

_____

_____

I AM EASILY ABLE
TO CREATE
WEALTH AND
ABUNDANCE
FOR MYSELF AND OTHERS.

CHAPTER 5

CREATING A POSITIVE RELATIONSHIP WITH MONEY

W e think about our relationships with our spouses, families, and friends, but oftentimes, we don't think about creating a relationship with money. Building this relationship, however, is an important piece to building wealth and becoming financially independent. Creating a great relationship with money is key to having money. This may seem a little out there to some, but I've seen time and time again how not having money is a result of your relationship with money or, really, a lack of relationship with money. I had a colleague once say to me, "Money isn't important to me." My jaw dropped, and I almost choked on my lunch.

How short-sighted to tell money it's not important to us if we want money to stick around!

It's important for us to acknowledge our thoughts and feelings about money. Money gets such a bad reputation, but we all want and need it. And when people think they want it, they also often believe this means they are greedy. Wanting money doesn't make you greedy in any shape or form. Money is a tool. A tool we use to not only get the things we desire but also to help others. We can give it to charity, improve our communities, and help out family members and so many other things that, without money, we simply cannot do.

However, when we say, "Money isn't important," we're essentially scaring money away from us. Imagine if you had a friend and you told them they weren't important to you. Do you think they'd stick around? Absolutely not, who would!? Ask yourself, do you want money to stick around and help you when you need it? Of course you do. You'd better not say it's not important to you, or guess what, you'll never have it.

Another phrase I hear my clients admit is, "I don't want to think about money." And yes, I get it. Money is not the end all be all. There are so many things that are important other than money. But you better believe if you don't think money is important or you don't ever want to think about money, you will live your life pushing money away and deflecting it. You will never live a life of financial abundance, experience financial security, and realize that having money is not all that bad. In fact, it's a blessing, a blessing you get to share with others as well as yourself. Money is a blessing that allows you to sleep better every night, knowing that you and your family are taken care of. Money makes the important things in life easier.

Why not start saying, "Money is important to me" or "I am so happy and grateful for the money I have." Try this: "I appreciate money so much, and I would love it to stick around and support me." Or maybe this: "I would love for money to create peace of mind for me, so I never have to worry about money again." Now, that is a different mindset. It does not at all mean you are greedy or think money is more important than people. But it does let money support you in a healthy and abundant way.

You'll notice I personify money through here and talk about it as if it were a person. I love to do this because it helps us treat money with a certain amount of respect and care. We are used to treating people we value with respect and care, so figuring money as if it were a person that you might call up and say, "Hey, thank you for supporting me," can foster a much better relationship and a healthy mindset around money.

One of my favorite financial gurus is Suze Orman. She always says, "People first, then money, then things." This is a perfect quote, and it really puts things in perspective.

As we discussed in the last chapter, our relationship with money goes back to our childhood. We witnessed our parents' relationship with money and probably picked up on their money relationship and attached ourselves to some of those beliefs with or without knowing it.

Many things we carry around as adults reflect something we witnessed or were told as a child, and your relationship with money is no different. However, as they say, becoming aware is the first step to any change. Once you are aware of what is affecting your personal wealth, then you can take steps to change it. In this chapter, we will work through a three-step plan to continue to help change your relationship with money and start on a new path to financial abundance.

Step One – Notice your words and your thoughts around money. If you can't witness them yourself, then ask a friend or family member or hire a coach to help you become aware. Once you are aware of your thoughts and feelings around money, you can change them. However, if you are not aware of it, it becomes hard to change. Once you start becoming aware, you will open the floodgates. Take a week or a few days, and every time you have a negative thought around money, write it down. Write in the space below:

_____

_____

_____

_____

_____

_____

_____

_____

_____

_____

_____

_____

_____

Here are a few examples of thoughts my clients have shared.

"I can't make ends meet."

"I can't afford ___." (fill in the blank)

"I wish I could afford _____."

"I don't have enough money to do ___."

"I'll never have enough money to have/buy ___."

"There is never anything left to save."

"I'm drowning in debt."

"I'm afraid I'll never be able to retire or have financial security."

I often hear women say, "I can't afford XYZ.'" Next time you want to say that you can't afford something, try saying, "I choose not to spend my money on 'XYZ.'" You see, most people take the disempowering road and say, "I can't afford it." Instead, try the empowering road and say the real reason you are making a choice and this is not the right choice for you at the moment.

Saying you can't afford something is disempowering, and it's also sending those messages to your brain of scarcity and lack. If you make a choice, then it's so much more empowering.

Choosing your words is everything. If you think about it, we can afford anything we want to afford. If the next day someone you love needed money for an operation and you were the only person who could help, and it was exactly the same amount that you would have spent on that "XYZ," chances are you'd find that money somewhere to help them out. We can almost always find money for things we feel are a must or important enough to us. So release the "I can't afford it" and commit to "I choose not to at this time."

Step Two – Write a letter to money as if money were a friend of yours (and it is!). This will help you heal your relationship with money. And, it's something you can go back to when you need to. In this letter, apologize for any time you've treated money badly, ignored money, didn't think money was important, or didn't give your money the time or attention it deserved.

Then tell money how you are going to start treating it better. Tell it how you are going to make money one of the most important things in your life. Tell it how you are going to make time for money and how you are going to take care of money. Share how you are going to be grateful for every amount of money that comes your way, no matter how small. Think of it as writing a letter to your best friend to whom you've not been a good friend to, and you want so badly to make up for any wrongdoings. Share how you will treat her so well going forward that she'll forget about all the past neglect. Tell your friend how you are going to take such good care of her and cherish her friendship. Write about how you will now be the best friend she ever had. I'm not a mushy, gushy person, but here I say, turn it up to full-blown mush! If you write this letter correctly, you should be crying by the end of it. Here are two examples:

Dear Money,

I hope this letter finds you well. I must begin by extending my sincerest apologies for the way I have treated you in the past. There have been times when I disregarded your importance, neglected your presence, and failed to give you the time and attention you truly deserve. For that, I am truly sorry.

You have always been by my side, supporting me in various ways, yet I took you for granted. I didn't realize the impact you can have on my life, and I failed to recognize the value you bring. But today, I want to make a change. I want to heal our relationship and transform it into something beautiful and prosperous.

From this moment forward, I pledge to treat you with the utmost respect and appreciation. I will make you one of the most important aspects of my life, recognizing the role you play in providing security, opportunities, and freedom. I will no longer underestimate your significance or ignore your presence.

I am committed to making time for you, Money. I will devote my efforts and energy to understanding how to manage you wisely. I will educate myself about personal finance, investments, and financial planning to ensure that I make the most of our partnership. I will be proactive in seeking opportunities to grow you and nurture our bond.

Gratitude will become an integral part of my relationship with you. No amount of money that comes my way, no matter how small, will go unnoticed or unappreciated. I will be thankful for every dollar that enters my life, recognizing its potential and the opportunities it can bring.

Money, I want to be the best friend you ever had. I want to take care of you, cherish our friendship, and nourish our connection. I promise to handle you responsibly, avoiding unnecessary debt and living within my means. I will prioritize saving and investing, ensuring a secure and prosperous future for both of us.

Together, we will achieve great things. I envision a life where we can make a positive impact on the world, where our resources can be utilized to support causes we believe in and help those in need. I will use you as a tool for good, making a difference in my own life and the lives of others.

Money, please accept my heartfelt apology and my sincere desire to make amends. I am committed to treating you with the love, respect, and care you deserve. Let us embark on this new journey together, knowing that our bond will grow stronger with each passing day.

With gratitude xoxo

Me.

Dear Money,

I hope this letter finds you well, and I want to begin by expressing my deepest apologies for the times I held onto you too tightly, doubting that you would come back to me. I confess that I have been guilty of clinging onto you out of fear, not fully trusting in your abundance and flow. For this, I am truly sorry.

Today, I stand before you with a newfound understanding and a desire to heal our relationship. I pledge to treat you with the respect, love, and trust that you deserve. I now realize that holding onto you tightly only limits your power and stifles the natural cycle of abundance.

Money, I want to make a heartfelt promise to treat you better. You will become one of the most important aspects of my life, not out of greed but out of a deep respect for the opportunities and freedom you can provide. I will release the grip of fear and embrace the belief that you will come back to me if I need to let you go for the greater good.

I commit to making time for you, Money. No longer will I neglect your presence or push you aside. I will dedicate myself to learning and understanding the intricacies of financial management. I will educate myself about investments, savings, and wise financial decisions. By empowering myself with knowledge, I will make better choices and create a life of stability and abundance.

Gratitude will become the foundation of our relationship. I will no longer overlook or dismiss the value of every amount of money that comes my way, no matter how small. I will greet each contribution with open arms, appreciating the opportunities they present and the doors they open. Every dollar will be a reminder of the potential and blessings you bring into my life.

Money, I want to be the friend you deserve, treating you with the utmost care and respect. I will embrace the understanding that our relationship is a symbiotic one, where I take care of you, and in turn, you take care of me. I will make conscious choices, avoiding unnecessary debt and wasteful spending. Together, we will create a foundation of financial stability and abundance.

I want to be the best friend you have ever had, Money. I will cherish and nurture our friendship, appreciating the profound impact you have on my life and the lives of those I care about. I will empower myself and other women to embrace their financial power, break free from limiting beliefs, and create a life of purpose and fulfillment.

Money, please accept my sincere apologies. I am committed to making amends and transforming our relationship into one of mutual respect, trust, and empowerment. Let us embark on this journey together, knowing that the future holds infinite possibilities.

With gratitude xoxo

Me.

Prompt: Now, write yours. Put aside any worry about it being corny and write a sincere, heartfelt letter to money.

Step 3 – Next, create a Prosperity and Abundance mantra around your new relationship with money and say it every day. A Prosperity and Abundance mantra is more than a set of words; it's a declaration of your intentions, beliefs, and desired relationship with finances. At its core, a good mantra should empower and uplift you, infusing you with positivity and a sense of control over your financial destiny. It's about gratitude for current blessings, optimism for what's to come, and confidence in your worthiness to receive wealth. While your mantra should resonate with your current beliefs, it can also be aspirational, pushing you slightly beyond your comfort zone to motivate you toward greater financial prosperity. As you recite this mantra, let it not only be words but also a means to shift any negative beliefs and open your mind to the boundless opportunities for wealth creation. Having a Prosperity and Abundance mantra is a crucial step to helping you change your relationship with money. Pick one for this exercise that sets the tone for the new relationship you want to have with money. You'll notice that there are mantras scattered throughout this book, as an example! I invite you to pick one that particularly resonates with you and use it as the wallpaper on your phone, tablet, or computer. For this exercise, I like to address these mantras directly to money to continue to help you figure your interactions with money as an important relationship in your life.

Here are some examples:

MONEY, I AM SO HAPPY AND GRATEFUL YOU SHOW UP
IN MY LIFE EVERY DAY IN INCREASING AMOUNTS.

MONEY, THANK YOU FOR CREATING THE SECURITY I NEED
TO HAVE PEACE OF MIND EVERY DAY IN MY LIFE.

MONEY, I TRULY APPRECIATE YOU AND I AM SO EXCITED
WHEN YOU APPEAR IN MY LIFE.

MONEY, THANK YOU FOR MAKING ME A MAGNET
THAT ATTRACTS WEALTH AND PROSPERITY.

MONEY, I AM GRATEFUL FOR THE ABUNDANCE
THAT YOU BRING TO ME AND THOSE AROUND ME.

MONEY, I AM SO HAPPY AND GRATEFUL FOR THE MONEY
MIRACLES THAT MANIFEST IN MY LIFE EVERY DAY.

MONEY, I AM OPEN TO RECEIVING YOU FROM MULTIPLE
SOURCES, IN BOTH EXPECTED AND UNEXPECTED WAYS
ON A CONTINUOUS BASIS.

Repeating your mantra regularly and wholeheartedly believing in its power is key to attracting financial abundance into your life. Mantras work by shaping your mindset, directing your thoughts and energy towards the positive aspects of money, and aligning your subconscious mind with the frequency of wealth and prosperity. When you constantly repeat a mantra, you are programming your mind to recognize and attract opportunities for financial success and wealth.

With patience, persistence, and a positive mindset, you will begin to witness the transformation of your financial reality. This mantra will help you manifest greater wealth, prosperity, and abundance in your life.

One Prosperity and Abundance mantra I started using on a daily basis is "Money comes to me on a continuous basis, through multiple sources in expected and unexpected ways." I put it on a sticky note and kept it close so I could see it and read it all the time. And it worked. When I started doing this, I started seeing money come in expected and unexpected ways. One of the unexpected ways was a tax refund for my husband's business. I made a mistake one year, and though I thought that I had filed his corporate return, I didn't go back into the software to see that there was a problem with it, and it was rejected. It was months later until I noticed this, so it was super late. The IRS gave me a $1,000 fine, which was upsetting, but there was nothing I could do since I was in the wrong. I paid the fine. Over a year later, when I started using that mantra on a daily basis, I received a check in the mail returning that fine to me with no explanation. I realized that this mantra stuff really works! I had originally learned about using mantras from a book I read by Bob Proctor, *"The Secret to Think and Grow Rich Revealed."* He is one of my favorite personal development authors. If you haven't read any of his books, I urge you to check them out. They are all wonderful!

Rachel's story perfectly encapsulates this concept. Rachel, who runs a successful marketing business, was part of my three-month group coaching program called "Financially Empowered Sisterhood."

In one session that focused on money mindset, Rachel came in with a mindset of scarcity. However, after participating in this exercise and implementing a Prosperity and Abundance mantra, she had a significant breakthrough.

Rachel had been burdened with the notion of being cash-strapped but soon discovered that she had overlooked her invoicing responsibilities. After our session, she added up her outstanding invoices and found she was owed a whopping $20K! This realization instantly transformed her mindset from scarcity to abundance.

Furthermore, Rachel adopted the powerful Prosperity and Abundance mantra: "Money comes easily and freely to me." As she echoed this mantra, her perspective began to shift. She started to embrace the notion of abundance, shedding her scarcity mentality. It wasn't that the resources were lacking; she needed to align her mindset to recognize and draw them in. This epiphany not only reshaped her mindset but also brought a positive change to her attitude and the energy she devoted to her business, sparking a profound transformation.

If you are not into using mantras, that's ok. I wasn't at first, either. To be perfectly honest, I thought it was all a bunch of bull. And then I tried it. As I've said, I am a numbers girl. I like things to be concrete, and I am not well-versed in the world of "woo." But I thought, what the heck, it sure can't hurt to try. What have I got to lose? Regardless of whether you want to try using mantras or not, creating a positive relationship with money is extremely important. I am sure you've heard the saying, "What we focus on grows." I'm sure you've heard it because it is the title of chapter two of this book! A reminder that there is a ton of truth to that saying. And if money isn't important to you or you don't want to think about it, well, I hate to break it to you, but you definitely need to come to terms with the fact that you probably won't have as much of it as you'd like.

Remember, when you start to think of money as your best friend, someone you love and cherish, someone who you know will always be there for you when you need them, someone who you get super excited to see every time they appear in your life, you'll see a significant difference in your life, money, and wealth. You'll start attracting money instead of deflecting it. It will make a huge difference to your financial health and well-being. And really, what have you got to lose by giving it a try?

MONEY
IS A TOOL FOR
CREATING
POSITIVE CHANGE
IN MY LIFE
AND THE WORLD.

CHAPTER 6

PLANNING FOR PROSPERITY WITH PATIENCE AND PERSISTENCE

I remember it like it was yesterday. I was sitting at my admin job with nothing to do, as usual. I had a terrible boss who wouldn't give me any work all day, then 30 minutes before it was time for me to go, he would throw a crap load of work at me and want me to finish it before I left. I hated that job, but that's a story for another day. I was recently married with no children yet. My husband and I were struggling to make ends meet. We owned a home that he actually bought before we were married, but had two roommates to help defer the costs. Now, he and I were trying to figure out how to afford this house together. We didn't make much. At that time, he was a machinist, and I was an administrative assistant. I had a car payment, and because I had been in an accident recently, my car insurance was ridiculously high. One day, in my free time at work, I decided to put all our income and expenses down on paper to see how it looked. Once I finished, I was in tears. How was it possible our monthly expenses, even without any fun or entertainment built in, were more than our income? It was so depressing that I ripped it up, and I never wanted to do that again. My husband was ready for children almost as soon as the ink was dry on our marriage license, but there was no way we could afford it. Especially after doing that monthly budget. I told him we couldn't afford children, and parenthood was off the table until we could figure out how to get out of the red on our monthly expenses.

He heard me loud and clear, and it wasn't long after that he decided to make some money on the side. He borrowed money from his parents, bought a commercial mower, and started cutting grass after work every day when he finished his job at 3 p.m. After he worked to pay his dad back for the mower, the extra money coming in did start to help. Since we didn't have any money to pay someone to do the bookkeeping, I taught myself to take care of this part of the business and actually enjoyed it. Having this extra income brought us a little sense of relief. This was also when I came across that Money Magazine article that started me on the path to investing $50 per month so we could start building a nest egg for ourselves.

Now, this is a chapter about creating a budget, or a Prosperity Blueprint as I prefer to call it. A plan tells your money where to go instead of letting it go wherever it wants. Having a plan for your money is super important. Think of trying to drive across the country without any sort of plan, GPS, or map. It would make it so much more difficult and frustrating to get where you wanted to go. However, I want to take a second to assure you that however depressing creating this budget may feel, it is worth it. No matter your circumstances, there is always a way out. You may need to be open to new opportunities and find ways to change, but you are capable. Have a growth mindset and try to be open to things you might not have been open to before. But first, knowing where you are now and what you are doing with your money is so important. Once you have it on paper, you can figure out what to do next so you can make some positive changes to your plan.

If you find you are in the red like I was, how can you figure out a way to make more money? Most of the women I coach are small business owners, which makes it a bit easier to increase their income or take on additional work than those who are in a 9-5 job. If you have a corporate job, there are always other opportunities, such as getting a new job, which often comes with increased pay. Or maybe you can do what my husband and I did (unknowingly at the time.) We started a side hustle that then, within two years, turned into a full-fledged business that he enjoyed more than his original job and made more money than that job, too. A side hustle is a great way to bring more income if you are in a 9-5 job.

And there are so many ways you can do this. Think about your marketable skills. Even if you think you have none, cutting grass as my husband did really didn't take much skill, just the willingness to work a bit harder and put in some extra time to make money. Sometimes, when your budget or plan is in the red, it leads to a great way out to a better life.

There are two ways to transition your plan into one that will allow you to start saving and investing. You must either increase your income or decrease your expenses. If decreasing your expenses sounds like the best way for you to go, think of things you can live without or cut down on in moderation. Can you switch from cable TV to internet TV? Can you cancel that gym membership you never really use anyway and start exercising at home? Try adding up the amount of money you spend each month eating out at restaurants or ordering delivery. Can you cut back there? Once you start tracking what you are spending, it's often eye-opening when you sit down and identify where all your money is going. Remember to take a look at those subscriptions for apps or streaming services you don't really use. Putting things down on paper (or in a Google Sheet) can help you see clearly. If you don't put it down on paper, you won't know where you stand or where your money is going. I've created a simple Google sheet called Prosperity Blueprint, which is a simple plan for you to use. It gives you an easy way, without being too overwhelming, to have a plan in place.

You can find a copy in the book portal.

I've had such a great response from my coaching clients on this sheet. They love it. Most say they've tried making a budget, and it felt too restrictive and time-consuming, but doing the Prosperity Blueprint felt so much better. One client, Jen, said, "This was great. You showed me how to change my future, and I feel hopeful about it."

I hope you have the same experience. Once you are able to put things down on paper and see it, it gives you amazing clarity. Clarity gives you peace of mind and a sense of security. If you prefer to create a blueprint on your own, here are the steps for you to follow.

Step One: Gather all your information. You can take a look at the last twelve months. I like to add up twelve months' worth of expenses and then divide it by twelve to get the monthly average. Now, if your income or expenses have changed in the last couple of months, you need to remember to factor that into the equation. Let's say you got a raise or purchased a new car in the more recent past, so of course, you'll factor that in. Also, there are often financial occurrences in the year that may only happen once, such as a tax return. Consider looking at both the entire year and also the last month or two and note any significant changes.

Step Two: Put it all together on a spreadsheet. Your income can be the average amount of income or deposits that hit your personal bank account. If you have a business, hopefully, you should have a personal bank account and a business bank account so it is clear which account is which. There are also other factors to consider if you have your own business. You will need to account for taxes in your expenses, but for now, take your net income and put it at the top, plus any net salary if you are taking a paycheck. If you are married, include your spouse's income too. This financial plan should be for both of you if you are married.

Next, put down your monthly fixed payments. This would be things like your mortgage payment, insurance, bills such as electric, phone, cable, gym, your second mortgage if you have one, taxes, student loans, car loans, etc. Include all your necessities and fixed monthly expenses. This does not include going out to eat, groceries, clothing or any variable or unnecessary expenses. Electricity is variable, but it is a necessity. Food and clothing are necessities, of course, but we often spend too much in these areas, so I have a separate section for those. I'll elaborate on this later.

Next, put in your monthly savings amounts. For example, $100 Mutual Fund, $100 Kids College Accounts, and $200 IRA/Retirement Accounts. This is where my Prosperity Blueprint is different. Most people try to use "what is left over" for their savings. In my Prosperity Blueprint, we save first. You want to take your income, subtract all your fixed expenses *and savings*, then you'll have a number that is left over. This is the money you can spend each month on food, clothing, and any other variable expenses that you did not include in your fixed expenses. I'll give you an example below.

PROSPERITY BLUEPRINT Example:

Monthly Payments	
Home Equity Line of Credit	$350.00
First Mortgage (Include RE Taxes, etc.) or Rent	$1,525.00
Taxes (business owners only)	$725.00
Electric/Utilities (12-month average)	$350.00
Insurance Car & House	$150.00
Cable/Internet	$100.00
Car Payment	$450.00
Gym	$35.00
Life Insurance	$90.00
Student Loan	$250.00
TOTAL:	**$4,025.00**

Savings:	
Personal Mutual Fund	$50.00
Kids College	$100.00
Retirement Savings	$200.00
TOTAL:	**$350.00**

What's Left Over (Take Income, then Subtract Monthly Expenses & Savings)	**$1,825.00**

The number that is left over after monthly payments and savings is what you can use as your food, clothing, and entertainment money. I suggest you put all of these expenses together on one credit card. This will make it easier for you to track this number. And make sure you pay it off *every month*. If you overspend and are paying interest on this, you will have less money in the "leftover" pot. Then you'll need to spend less the next month so you can make up for the shortage the month before.

Again, notice how we are treating the savings as a bill here, and we spend "what's left over." Throughout my life, ever since that Money Magazine article I read, I've always treated savings as part of my plan, part of my budget. I treated savings like an electric bill that I had to pay. I never looked at savings as I'll save what's left over, as I often hear from women who come to me for business financial coaching. If I did look at savings that way, not only would I not achieve the financial success I have, but I would be jeopardizing my dreams and vision for the life I wanted to live. That is why we started with the dream and anchored it with our "why" in Chapter One.

Oftentimes, women I coach say, "There is nothing left over, so how can I save anything?" And here is where I coach differently. I coach the women to make savings "non-negotiable." To set up a goal for savings, create a "why" behind it and then put it on auto-debit. This is how I've done it my entire life. And when I set a new goal, I re-look at my auto-debit and adjust it accordingly. For a girl whose mother repeatedly told her, "Money burns a hole in your pocket," I did pretty well at building my wealth. Although there were key things I needed to change in my mindset first, of course. One of them was having a goal or a dream to save for, and the other was saving like it was a necessity, not an option. Having a "why" behind the goal is critical. It makes it so much easier to devote resources rather than to save for the sake of saving.

Recently, a client asked me, "What if I called saving a "self-love" bill? It is a non-negotiable bill that would automatically come out of my account, no matter what, as a show of love. It is the love I am giving to myself and my future." What a great way to think about it: Loving yourself enough to set up the security and peace of mind for your future.

Step Three - Now take a long, hard look at the amount of "leftover" money. Do you really need this much every month for the rest of your expenses? Can you possibly increase your savings? If you are not saving any money, now you can see clearly how much you are spending every month on your monthly payments. And if there is nothing you can reduce in your monthly payments, that's ok. Where most people need help is in the "other" column. In the example above, this person is spending 29% of their monthly income in the "other" category while their savings is only 6%. I recommend trying to keep your "other" spending to 10% of your income and to match your savings to at least that amount, saving 10% of your net income in some way.

In this example, I would have my client look at all their "other" expenses and see if they can cut back anywhere. I would advise them to gradually increase their savings and decrease their other expenses and aim for getting the "other" down by 8-10% and their savings up by 8-10%. Oftentimes, when we see it all down on paper, it makes it easy to see exactly where we can make changes.

I know all of this can be very overwhelming and intimidating at times. What I suggest is trying to find the easiest path for you, whether it be increasing your income or decreasing your expenses. A mentor of mine, Sara Connell, has a great exercise she does with her clients. It's called "50 Ways." She has her clients write down 50 ways they can increase their income. Even if you are not a small business owner, there are at least 50 ways you can make more money. For example, you could sell items you own online that you don't use anymore. (That treadmill that doubles as a clothes rack is a good example). Or, you could increase your rates. If you are a small business owner or you are paid for services, can you increase your rates a little? How recently have you increased the cost of your time? Remember that the cost of your time should go up according to the level of your experience, so if it has been a while since your rates increased, it is likely time to do so. A little increase adds up to a lot over a year without any additional work or effort.

I AM GRATEFUL
FOR THE ABUNDANCE OF
WEALTH AND
OPPORTUNITIES
AVAILABLE TO ME.

As I mentioned before, I often coach female business owners. And I can vouch for the fact that most female business owners under charge for their services. Why do women do this so often? So many of us have such fear around charging our value. I was no exception to this when I first started. In fact, I was a perfect example of not charging my value.

When I started my consulting/coaching business, I left a full-time job as a Controller/CFO to do so. My boss and I discussed staying on in a consulting role. Since I was stepping away without any clients, I was excited to have my former boss as a client to help support me financially right off the bat. I did some math and gave him a rate of $60 per hour, which was basically my salary reconfigured into a consulting fee. I also said I would increase that rate to $70 an hour after three months, as I gave him time to find some additional help in-house and cut back my hours. After about a year, I realized I had attracted a few more clients at a much higher rate than I was charging him. These new clients didn't seem to think my new fee was high at all. This is when I realized I was considerably undercharging him for my services. At this point, I also now have my MBA. When I went to speak with him about going from an hourly rate to a flat fee consulting rate, which would have also increased the monthly amount he was paying me, it didn't go so well. We ended up parting ways. At the time, I was a bit upset that I lost my largest client, but it turns out that this decision opened up space for bigger, better, higher-paying clients who knew my value and could appreciate my worth.

Since then, I've raised my rate several times, and it always lands me better clients. Once, I doubled my consulting rate almost overnight by trying it out on a new client that I knew could afford my higher rate. It was a multi-eight-figure business that really needed my help and expertise. And guess what? He didn't bat an eyelash at the rate I quoted him. Once I saw how easy it was to raise my rate, that became my standard rate for new clients, again, almost double what I had been charging.

Here's a secret I'd love to share with you: You don't have to have a seven-figure business to create a seven-figure net worth. I didn't have a seven-figure business when I created a seven-figure net worth. I had a profitable six-figure business. And a seven-figure business does not, at least in my view, make you a millionaire unless you can sell that business for seven figures and step away from it completely. And you can have a seven-figure business and be making no profit. This happens often. It's better to have a six- or multi-six-figure business and be making a good profit and investing your money than a seven-figure business that isn't showing a profit.

It is important to keep in mind that even if you have a profitable seven-figure business, it could always potentially disappear overnight. If you're not investing some of your earnings personally as a backup plan or safety net, you could be in trouble. We saw that happen to so many businesses during the Covid-19 pandemic. Consider what happened to many taxicab companies when ridesharing apps like Uber and Lyft became the norm. I don't mean to scare you or imply that your business will cease to exist, but I do want to impress upon you that it is essential to have a backup plan, no matter how successful your business is. You still need to build a nest egg to create financial protection for you and your family. It is important to create a financial security blanket in case something happens, or in case you become injured or ill and can't run your business, or if one of your children, spouse, or parent became seriously ill and you had to take time off to care for them. Wouldn't it be nice to know you have a backup plan for any of these unforeseen circumstances? Wouldn't that give you a sense of peace and security?

Once you create your Prosperity Blueprint, you'll know exactly what your monthly "nut" is. That's what I like to call the amount of revenue you need to earn each month to "keep the lights on." Everything else over that is gravy - aka profit. If you figure out your personal "nut," if something unexpected happens, you know exactly how much it will cost you to keep your family's "lights on" and feel supported during your personal time of need. While we can never be fully prepared for the implications of a "what if," not having to do this calculation if something goes amiss will remove at least one burden from that experience.

What happens when your goal seems too big, too overwhelming, or too scary? What if your goal is to save for your child's education, and you can't see it happening, and it often feels defeating? I know exactly where you are coming from. I tried to plan out saving for my children's education. When I actually started looking at the cost of college and what I wanted to be able to help them with, I had so much anxiety. My goal was always for them to put a little skin in the game, so they came out with a small loan, something closer to a car payment rather than the kind of student debt that looks more like a mortgage payment. I told my children their college budget was $30K per year, and they had to find a school that either cost that or less. After I made that decision, I quickly realized that there would be one year that all three children would be in college. That meant $90K that year in tuition. With their student loans, they would each need a little closer to 20k in tuition, but still! How was I possibly going to afford $70+K in tuition that year? What was I thinking? What was I thinking when I had three children less than four years apart? Obviously not about college.

I would open up my spreadsheet and do this math all the time and close it again with more anxiety and no solutions. At that time, my gross salary was only $80K before taxes. My husband had his business and brought in money, but we needed that money to live on. At the time, I was told that if you made $100K joint income, you'd get no financial aid. This haunted me for years, and every time I opened up my spreadsheet, there was no way I could make that year work, no way I could possibly afford that year. Well, guess what? That year never happened. My oldest two children left college before my youngest even entered college. My oldest son went back to college later but commuted to a local college that was inexpensive. And my middle son quit college to go to a trade school instead. All that anxiety I put myself through, and it never even happened!

How many times do we do this with all sorts of different scenarios in our lives? We worry about something that then never even comes to pass. Yes, it's great to have a plan, but learn from my experience, and don't stress yourself out over what could potentially happen. Life has a funny way of working out in your favor. Things don't always happen the way we think they will. Often, God or the Universe, whichever you prefer, has our back, and everything comes together just fine. Or, we get creative and we figure out a solution. Either way, you're often taken care of.

Remember, you are always going to hit roadblocks along the way or have a defeated feeling when something difficult happens. You may get thrown off track for a little while. But as long as you stay the course, go back and redo your plan, and always make saving a priority, you'll be able to make a significant difference in your future and for the future of those you love. The key to all of it is to have a plan, work the plan, and be patient and persistent when achieving your financial goals. We all want a quick fix, that magic pill to take to make it all better, or some unknown aunt or uncle to leave us a large inheritance. The perhaps less glamorous but much more useful solution is slow and steady, staying the course and following the financial path to prosperity. Financial independence is a long-term game, and the best way to achieve it is by continually educating yourself. Knowledge is power, and persistence has a big payoff. Having a plan is priceless!

*Prompt: Create your **Prosperity Blueprint!***

Monthly Payments

_____

TOTAL:

Savings:

_____

TOTAL:

What's Left Over (Take Income, then Subtract Monthly Expenses & Savings)

WEALTH

IS A TOOL
THAT CAN BE USED
TO HELP OTHERS.

CHAPTER 7

EMBRACING YOUR MONEY PERSONALITY

I've always been curious why some people are savers and others are not. Is it upbringing? I think I can rule that one out because I have three children, and they are all very different in their saving and spending habits. So, if it isn't upbringing, what is it that makes us all different in our habits?

A few years ago, I decided to become DISC-certified. If you are not familiar with DISC, it is a testing method used to understand and categorize different personality traits and behaviors. It is based on the DISC model, which stands for Dominance, Influence, Steadiness, and Conscientiousness. In simple terms, the DISC model helps us understand how people tend to act and communicate in different situations and helps enhance our self-awareness. Soon after becoming certified, I realized that I could attribute these same traits to how people spend and save money.

On the next several pages, we'll walk through the four Money Behavior Styles that I created. Here, you'll find ways to identify and improve your natural tendencies around spending and saving, see what profiles resonate with you, and find which styles are dominant for you.

You may find you have more than one dominant style. Some people, like me, have as many as three dominant styles! If you only have one dominant style, it will be easier to utilize the suggestions I provide to strengthen your money style. If you think you have more than one, be sure to study all the styles that you feel are dominant and relevant to you and use suggestions you connect with most to strengthen your style. The information listed for each style will help you notice your natural spending and saving tendencies and help you elevate your approach to savings, investing, and spending, enabling you to make more informed, intentional, and rewarding financial decisions and grow your wealth. Keep in mind that everyone has some of every style in them. We're looking for your dominant or "high" style or styles that feel like *you* in order to give you insight into your money behavior that is natural to you.

DISC ASSESSMENT

DOMINANT/
DECISIVE

DOMINANT/DECISIVE MONEY STYLE (D)

Dominant/Decisive money styles are quick to act and make decisions. I like to compare the high D styles to a tiger. A tiger is a symbol of strength and determination. High D's, like tigers, are decisive with their actions but can have occasional impulsiveness. High Ds are assertive and, at times, relentless, as well as competitive. Oftentimes, they are fearless and will do anything to overcome limitations to achieve excellence. Like tigers, high D's are risk-taking by nature and will go beyond their comfort zones, but they sometimes desire quick results and often lack patience. This style usually embodies the power of extraordinary courage and confidence to all.

If you are a high D, you'll often notice the following behavior traits.

- Make decisions quickly
- Action Taker
- Assertive
- Competitive
- May bend or break rules
- Goal Oriented
- Impulsive
- Logic driven

When it comes to savings and investing, you may have a fearless attitude towards risk-taking, always seeking opportunities with the potential for quick returns. Your curiosity drives you to stay ahead of the curve, constantly exploring the latest and greatest possibilities in investing.

While your fearless attitude has its advantages, it's important to recognize the disadvantages as well. You can be impatient and might favor immediate gains over long-term successes. Sometimes, this impatience can lead to missed opportunities that could have offered substantial returns given enough time.

As for your typical spending habits, your impulsive nature can lead to spontaneous purchases. Your desire for the latest and greatest products and services drives you to constantly seek out new and innovative offerings in the market.

It's important to take a step back sometimes to strengthen and upgrade your tendencies as a dominant/decisive money style. When it comes to investing and growing your wealth, remind yourself that it's a long-term game. Try to be patient and resist the urge to make quick decisions based only on short-term gains.

When making purchases, especially large ones, it's key to take time to evaluate and avoid impulsive decisions. Take a few days or even a week to evaluate whether the purchase aligns with your long-term financial plans and goals. This will allow you to make better decisions and avoid buyer's remorse.

Additionally, think about engaging your intuition and consider how you genuinely feel about a potential purchase or investment opportunity. While logic and analysis are important, don't underestimate the power of your intuition. Trust your instincts and consider the emotional aspect of your decision-making process. By striking a balance between logic and intuition, you can make choices that not only make financial sense but also resonate with your personal values and aspirations.

DISC ASSESSMENT

INFLUENCE/INSPIRING MONEY STYLE (I)

People with an Influence/Inspiring Money Style have an optimistic and trusting money style. If I's were represented by an animal, they would be a butterfly. People who are high I's are motivating and often encourage us to believe in ourselves. High Is have the gift of filling others with excitement and positivity. High I's can be friendly and don't tend to follow rules. Like the butterfly transforms from a caterpillar, High I's inspire us to grow, evolve, and thrive. If you are a high I, you'll often have the following behavior traits.

- Inspiring
- Optimistic
- Social
- Charming
- Persuasive
- Rule breaker
- Fun/Entertaining
- Creative
- Trusting
- Motivating

Being the kind of person who is motivated by helping others and saving specifically for their benefit brings advantages. Your selflessness and generosity can create stronger relationships and a sense of purpose. Although, it can also prevent you from putting your own financial goals first. I's tend to get caught filling other people's cups before they fill their own. It's crucial to strike a balance between supporting others and ensuring your own financial security.

When it comes to spending, your motivations revolve around status and fun. What matters most to you is how a purchase makes you feel. It's important for you to find a balance between indulging in enjoyable purchases and practicing mindful spending.

Several strategies can strengthen and upgrade your spending tendencies. First, try practicing mindfulness when you go to make a purchase. Before making a purchase, pause and ask yourself if it's something you truly need or if it aligns with your long-term financial goals.

By being more intentional with your spending, you can avoid impulsive purchases, begin to grow your wealth and create a path to financial security for you and your loved ones. Remind yourself of that greater goal.

Additionally, make investing a fun and engaging activity. Instead of viewing it as a mundane task, create a game with yourself to see how much you can grow your wealth. Set goals, track your progress, and celebrate milestones along the way. This approach can make investing more enjoyable and motivate you to continue building your financial future.

You may also consider finding an accountability partner or joining a group. This can help you stay on track and make more informed choices while indulging your fun and social side. It will also strengthen your financial habits so you can develop a more balanced approach to managing your money.

DISC ASSESSMENT

STEADINESS/
SUPPORTING

STEADINESS/SUPPORTING MONEY STYLE (S)

Those with a S Money Style are steady and supportive. They have a stable and loyal money style. And if you were an animal, you would be a dog.

High S's are sincere. Think of how dogs always show their true feelings and love us no matter what. High S's, like dogs, are incredibly supportive and loyal, always sticking by our side. They bring consistency to our lives with their routines, making us feel safe and secure. When we're stressed, high S's have a magical calmness that brings us peace. High S's are also super friendly, making new friends wherever they go and easily making everyone feel special. Their patience is truly remarkable.

If you are a high S, you'll often have the following behavior traits.

- Sincere
- Supportive
- Loyal
- Consistent
- Calm
- Stable
- Patient

With this money style, you prefer security and gradual progress, which brings several advantages. By prioritizing savings, you will build a strong financial safety net that can provide peace of mind and a sense of stability. With you, slow and steady wins the race. You make careful and well-thought-out financial decisions. Also, your desire to benefit others is truly admirable. Your commitment to security, gradual progress, and helping others creates a financially stable environment.

One potential drawback is that your aversion to risk may limit your opportunities for financial growth. Another disadvantage is that your emphasis on benefiting others may sometimes overshadow your own financial needs.

Spending is a cautious and thrifty approach for you. Your mindset revolves around being careful with your expenses and making practical choices. Your selfless nature shines through as you prioritize the needs and happiness of those around you.

Here are a few strategies you can consider to strengthen your natural tendencies. First, explore the possibility of taking a few more risks in your investments. While it's important to maintain a level of caution, being open to slightly more risky ventures can provide opportunities for greater financial growth and higher returns.

Also, remember to occasionally treat yourself and buy things for yourself rather than always prioritizing others. Because you know that you have managed your finances well, you can afford to occasionally treat yourself without impacting your financial stability.

Lastly, be open to new opportunities and embrace change. Being willing to try new things can lead to exciting ventures and financial growth. Seek out new opportunities that may enhance your financial well-being. By incorporating these strategies into your financial mindset, you can strengthen and upgrade your tendencies and bring balance, growth, and a sense of fulfillment to your financial journey.

DISC ASSESSMENT

CONSCIENTIOUS/ CAUTIOUS

CONSCIENTIOUS/CAUTIOUS MONEY STYLE (C)

Those with a C Money Style are often cautious and conservative when it comes to money. They have a skeptical but analytical money style. If they were an animal, they would be a fox.

High C's, like the fox, are known to have some amazing traits. They are very careful and always watchful to avoid danger. High C's also follow rules and get along well with others in their community. When faced with challenges, high C's think carefully and consider different ways to solve the problem. High Cs, like foxes, often use their cleverness to outsmart any challenges. Their movements are precise, and they pay close attention to small details. High C's are cautious, follow the rules, think carefully, and do things with great care and precision.

If you are a high C, you'll often have the following behavior traits.

- Conservative
- Cautious
- Detailed
- Precise
- Rule Follower
- Analytical
- Logical

When it comes to saving money, your preference is for guarantees and relying on logical thinking. Your logical and analytical mindset helps you make well-informed decisions based on careful research. This approach gives you confidence and a sense of security. Your responsible and careful saving habits set a strong foundation for long-term financial stability and a bright financial future. By focusing on guarantees and security, however, you can miss out on higher returns offered by riskier investments. Sometimes, your logical approach may cause you to overlook opportunities that require more intuitive decision-making.

When it comes to spending money, you have a thoughtful and meticulous approach. You evaluate every purchase carefully. You often have a strong preference for guarantees and will seek out reviews to guide your decision-making process. With your analytical mindset, you approach purchases with logic and reason.

To strengthen and upgrade your money management tendencies, it's important to remember to take calculated risks. While it's natural to prioritize security, taking some risks can potentially lead to higher returns and greater financial growth.

Be sure to consider limiting the amount of time you spend analyzing purchases. It's essential to remember that time is money. Avoid overthinking and getting caught in analysis paralysis. Set a reasonable timeframe for decision-making, weigh the pros and cons, and rely on your intuition to guide you. Trust yourself to make informed choices without getting bogged down in excessive comparison.

Try to be open to new opportunities that haven't been extensively tested and analyzed yet. By embracing new possibilities, you open yourself up to potentially rewarding opportunities. By incorporating these strategies into your financial approach, you can strengthen and upgrade your tendencies and find the right balance between analysis and action, the key to optimizing your financial success.

I AM CAPABLE
OF BECOMING
WEALTHY
WHILE REMAINING
TRUE TO MY
VALUES AND INTEGRITY.

Now that you are familiar with the different DISC money styles and how to uplevel your tendencies, I'd like you to commit to taking action! Ready? Let's do it!

Step One: *Identify what your most prominent DISC style is. Which one feels most like you when it comes to money?*

My most dominant DISC style is:

_____

The animal that represents my DISC style is:

_____

The strengths of my DISC style are:

_____

_____

_____

The weaknesses of my DISC Style are:

_____

_____

_____

Step Two: From this self-analysis, identify one thing you could do to improve your money management based on your DISC style. What is one thing you can do today to change and improve your natural tendencies around money?

_____

_____

_____

_____

_____

_____

_____

_____

_____

_____

_____

_____

Step Three: Commit to acting on one thing today.

_____

_____

_____

_____

_____

_____

_____

_____

_____

_____

_____

_____

_____

In order to show you how understanding your DISC style can improve your financial well-being and give you some understanding of your natural tendencies, I've included some examples below from clients of mine. I think you'll find their DISC-style journeys to be profound. I hope these empower you to take your understanding of your natural financial style to the next level!

Rachel's Journey: Learning to Value Herself

Meet Rachel, who is a high I and S in DISC and a business owner who loves helping others build their businesses. You'll recall that this makes her like a butterfly or a dog in her natural financial tendencies (picture a dog with butterfly wings- cute!) She has a successful marketing agency with a team that adores her. She's a friendly and powerful leader, always thinking about what's best for everyone, especially her clients. When we identified her DISC style, she realized she always put the client first, even when it came to money and charging for her and her team's services. That is where we found the problem. Rachel realized she wasn't charging enough for her services. She found herself adjusting her prices because she believed her clients needed the financial break. She realized she was always giving but not taking care of herself and her and her business's financial security.

When Rachel shared her feelings in my FES group, she quickly realized that it's okay to value herself and ask for what she and her team deserve. In fact, it is necessary! Immediately, Rachel started setting fair prices for her work and valuing it regardless of what she believed her clients could afford. She realized that being caring didn't mean she had to devalue herself and her team's work. Rachel learned you can balance kindness with charging appropriately. This has allowed Rachel to continue to grow her business and create financial security for her and her family.

Dina's Discovery: Taking Care of You Too

Say hello to Dina, who, like Rachel, is also a high I and S in DISC. Dina is a wonderful and successful realtor in Southwest Florida. She loves taking risks and looking out for others, but she had a habit of putting herself last, even with money. She would spend money on her family and friends but often forgot to take care of herself. While she was participating in the FES group, Dina quickly realized she could increase her mother's wealth by moving her accounts around in a way that would show an annual increased income of $17,000 for her mother. This is the very giving S part of Dina that shows up often. She was a pro at taking care of others. When Dina shared her story in the FES group, however, she realized that she was always looking out for her loved ones and rarely took the time to think about building her own wealth. She realized in the group she wasn't alone and that many other people struggled with this, too.

Eventually, Dina concluded that taking care of herself wasn't selfish. She learned she needed to start looking after herself and balance it with the needs of others. With this new understanding, Dina started saving money for herself as a stepping stone to building her own wealth. Her story inspired others in the group to do the same!

Louise's Balance Act: Making Choices Together

Louise, a prominent human resources consultant and leadership coach in the UK, is a high I and D in DISC (now picture a tiger with butterfly wings- also so cute!) She is a quick decision-maker who isn't afraid of risks. Sometimes, her choices clash with her husband's cautiousness. This caused some disagreements. Louise talked about this in the FES group, where she learned something important.

Louise discovered that making decisions together was crucial. She realized that combining her fast choices with his careful thinking could bring harmony to her decisions and her relationship. Louise agreed that her husband's cautiousness was actually the balance she needed to keep her from making rash decisions that she didn't take the time to think through when it came to money. She decided to be a bit more open-minded with her husband and listen to his reasoning when it came to their finances. She became aware that he could help her create the balance she needed to avoid any quick, risky endeavors that maybe she didn't think all the way through. He would also remind her to have patience when it came to growing their own wealth.

Her fiery, risk-taking nature could also balance out his slower, more cautious approach. Louise was able to find a way to create harmony in her relationship with her husband by embracing his own money style and realizing that rather than being opposites, they were actually compliments.

Morgan's Journey: Embracing Change

Morgan is a thoughtful and kind business powerhouse who has a successful social media business as well as an MLM (Multi-Level Marketing) business. She is a high C and S in DISC and a careful thinker who likes to take things slow. She would be represented by a fox or a dog, a natural combination. She always put in a lot of thought before spending money, but she also wanted to be a bit riskier when it came to investing and seeking higher returns. In FES, Morgan talked about this struggle.

Morgan realized that she could be both careful and daring. She began to take small risks with her money, using her thoughtful side to guide her. By the end of the program, she started investing a little bit of money every month. Morgan learned that change could be exciting and safe and that she could take a little bit of risk and still feel secure.

In these stories, you can see how knowing your DISC profile can help you understand your money behaviors and make positive changes. Perhaps you're like Rachel, an enthusiastic helper who sometimes undervalues yourself, or Dina, a risk-taker who puts others first. Learning from these stories, pinpoint one thing you can change to improve your natural tendencies.

Here, I'll remind you of your commitment to act on this one thing today. You can make a positive shift to shape and balance your financial future to build your wealth, and you can start now. It could be as simple as setting fair prices like Rachel did in order to take care of her and her business's financial needs. It may be prioritizing self-care in the form of starting to save and invest for yourself like Dina and Morgan did. And like Louise, maybe it's finding the balance between impulsiveness and logic. Once you identify your DISC money behavior, you gain the power to shift some of your natural tendencies and find balance.

Commit to these changes and take the first steps today. Share your goal with someone you trust, or consider joining a supportive community such as my Financial Empowerment Sisterhood (FES) for encouragement and help to guide your progress!

If you want to take an additional quiz and find out more about your specific DISC behavior profile, follow the code below. For a small fee, you'll get a full 40-page report (40 pages on you! Yes, you!) all about your DISC behaviors and how they connect to everything in your life, not only money.

Follow the Code to the FREE Book Portal.

By understanding your money behavior styles, you're equipped with the knowledge to make informed choices about your money. It's not about changing who you are but about leveraging your strengths and improving your financial well-being. Just like Rachel, Dina, Louise, and Morgan, you can shape a brighter financial future too.

In the world of personal finance, knowledge truly is power. Embrace this power, and let it guide you toward financial success and empowerment.

WEALTH IS AN

ABUNDANT RESOURCE

THAT CAN BE SHARED

BY EVERYONE.

CHAPTER 8

EMOTIONAL BUYING
- DISTINGUISHING FEELINGS VS. FINANCES

What is emotional buying? Emotional buying is a concept that, in many ways, mirrors the idea of emotional eating. It's an impulse that stems from our deepest feelings, driving us to purchase not out of need but as a reaction to our emotions, similar to how we might comfort ourselves with food after a hard day. Over the years, I've observed countless clients, friends, and even witnessed my own behavior swayed by this phenomenon.

One sunny afternoon, as I lounged by the pool with my friend Lynn, she told me all about a recent shopping spree.

"This year, I went overboard for my daughter's birthday," she confessed, her voice tinged with guilt. "She had such a challenging year, and I wanted to bring her some joy." While I kept my thoughts to myself, I recognized this as classic comfort, or emotional, buying. It's an all-too-familiar pattern: in challenging times, we often shower ourselves or loved ones with gifts, hoping to wash away that discomfort for the "high" of getting something new. This isn't entirely our fault- we're subject to countless advertisements per day that convince us that buying the next newest thing will be the ticket to happiness. The concerning aspect of Lynn's revelation, however, was not her own behavior but the unintentional lesson she might be sharing with her daughter. The idea that material purchases can heal us emotionally—a belief popularly termed "retail therapy"—can often lead us astray, encouraging us to acquire items without good reason or need.

But there's more than one way we buy things because of our emotions. Here are the four main types of emotional buying:

- The aforementioned comfort buying: purchasing things when we're sad or upset.
- FOMO (Fear of Missing Out) buying: When we think everyone else has something and, therefore, we should too.
- Fear buying: buying when we're scared of what might happen if we don't make the purchase.
- Impulse buying: When we buy something without really thinking it through.

A good example of FOMO buying was my experience deciding to invest in an in-ground pool. I recall it vividly! A couple of friends of mine installed in-ground pools, and because I saw theirs, I wanted one as well. I felt like I was missing out on this amazing thing they all had. I persuaded my reluctant husband and moved forward with a home equity loan to accomplish my dream of having an in-ground pool. A pool had always been something I'd wanted, but I never thought we'd have the financial ability to have one. Between that and the pressure I felt when seemingly all my friends were updating their yards with sparkly new pools, I decided to go for it. I completely knew it probably wouldn't be the best use of the equity in my home, but I did it anyway. Pools in our area don't really add any value to the home. But, determined to have a pool like my friends did, I moved forward. And $70K all in later, after the pool, concrete deck, landscaping, and fence, there she was - the most beautiful pool I had ever seen. I loved that pool, and we did get quite a bit of use out of it with friends and hosting parties while the kids were young. However, if I had that one to do all over again, I probably wouldn't have invested in getting a pool. I might have waited, taken a step back from the FOMO I was having and thought about it for a year to see if I was still in the same mindset.

I didn't realize at the time that the pool also cost us close to $2,000 per year for opening, closing, chemicals, and electricity. Fast forward 15 years, the kids have left home, it doesn't get much use, and both my husband and I totally hate taking care of it. While the pool hosted numerous memorable moments, in hindsight, it was an expenditure driven more by emotion and FOMO than anything else.

Fear is another emotional buying trigger many marketers like to use. Insurance or warranty purchases are perfect examples. Any kind of insurance or warranty is selling on the idea of fear. My husband's business insurance serves as a striking example. For three decades, he funneled $1,000 monthly into this insurance, amounting to a staggering $300,000 over the years—all without a single claim. From a legal standpoint, insurance was essential. But what if we had saved and invested that money instead? By my calculations (and I used my handy investment inspiration calculator for this), we could have had a whopping $2 million in an investment account by now. Consider that many forms of insurance or warranty purchases aren't mandatory. If the total cost of the insurance over the years is less than that money might be worth if invested, it doesn't really make much sense! If you're considering purchasing insurance or a warranty, play around with my investment inspiration calculator here to see how that money might benefit you instead:

The same consideration applies to life insurance as well. Back when I was in my late twenties, I got a whole life policy. But when I learned more about money and investing, I made a switch to term life. Whole life costs way more, but they say you get money from it if you don't pass away. After doing some number crunching, I saw that if I put the money I saved by switching from whole to term into a mutual fund, I'd end up with a lot more in the bank. The difference in the policy was $25 per month less. If I had paid the additional $25 per month and lived until I was 80 years old, I would have had a payout of $126,000. If I took that $25 per month and invested it instead at a rate of return of 10% when I was 80, I would have approximately $250,000, almost double what the insurance company payout was going to be.

And I still had the life insurance of $100,000 in case something happened to me before then. So that's what I did: switched and invested in the difference.

There are many other fear-type purchases people make. Most salespeople are trained to invoke fear into you to close the deal. For instance, in the real estate industry, agents might highlight the rapid pace of market growth to create a fear of missing out on a good investment.

In the auto industry, salespeople might bring up concerns regarding the safety features of older models to encourage the purchase of a new vehicle with advanced safety technologies. In the coaching world, I often hear, "I will get you to five-figure months if you buy my program or invest in my coaching." Often, if we don't see five-figure months or whatever was promised, that coach then turns the conversation around to blame you or your commitment to the program.

This type of selling infuriates me now, especially because there was a time when I bought into these programs based on false promises, scared I wouldn't achieve the results I wanted if I didn't sign up immediately. I am now a bit more immune to these types of sales pitches and often steer away from any fear-based selling strategies.

Next, let's address impulse buying. Ever been swept up by that rush of "I want this now?" You're not alone. You walk into a store for three items but walk out with a bag of ten. (I'm looking at you, Target!) Sound familiar? Of course, it does. That's the magic of stores placing those irresistible goodies right within our easy reach. They've got our number, and they're playing our tune.

Take Amazon, for example. They're pros at luring us into quick buys. With their "one-click" option, you barely have time to second guess. Boom! And, just like that, your order is on its way. And if you've got their app, it's even easier. They suggest products tailored to our past buys, making it feel like a shopping spree without even leaving our couch. Oh, and let's not forget the luxury of doorstep delivery in two days. Genius, right? While this convenience is amazing, let's face it, we've got to be smart. Just because it's a breeze to buy doesn't mean we should be tapping "add to cart" on every shiny thing we see.

I CAN LEARN
FROM THE HABITS
AND MINDSET OF
WEALTHY PEOPLE TO
CREATE ABUNDANCE
IN MY OWN LIFE.

So what can you do to stop emotional buying in its tracks and start building your wealth?

Follow these steps to empower yourself around emotional buying.

1. Reflect Before You Buy: Every time you're tempted to make a purchase, ask yourself:

- Is this truly necessary?
- Does this align with my financial goals and vision?
- Am I getting this to try to feel better or because I think that everyone else has it?

Understanding your motivations can prevent regretful decisions. Answering the above questions can empower you to make better decisions.

2. Strive for Balance: Create a strategy that nudges you towards your financial targets without being too restrictive. This might mean being thrifty in some areas so you can splurge in others. It's not about abandoning all your pleasures but rather making intelligent choices that propel you towards your desired financial destination. It's fine to indulge in what you want, not only what you need. Again, think of it in terms of eating: occasionally treating yourself ensures you don't feel deprived, which can lead to bigger binges later. If you enjoy getting your nails done, plan for it. Maybe alternate between at-home sessions and salon visits. The key is to find that sweet balance and have a strategy to achieve your financial aspirations.

3. Keep Your Eye on the Prize: Always recall the larger financial goal you've set. Look back at your plans and your vision board. Whenever you're about to buy something, challenge yourself: "Is this purchase going to delay my progress? Will it postpone my dream?" Weigh the urgency and necessity of the purchase against the gratification of the bigger goal.

After considering the above, if you've thoroughly weighed every option and still genuinely crave or require that item, don't deny yourself. Life isn't merely black and white—it's a colorful mosaic of choices, and occasionally, that includes indulging in our desires. However, ensure your purchases align with both your budget and aspirations. Embrace your purchases that bring joy without guilt, but also without letting them become a shadow for financial anxieties or an impediment to your larger objectives. It's not about giving up joys but about spending with purpose and intent. Having a flexible budget that acknowledges both necessities and pleasures allows you to cherish your purchases while still advancing toward your financial milestones.

SHE GROWS RICH

Let's go through some examples!

Imagine this: it's been a long, tough week. You're feeling drained, and you're looking for a pick-me-up. Then, an email notification pings on your phone – it's a sale from your favorite clothing store. An image of a bright, trendy outfit catches your eye, and you can almost feel your spirits lift.

You pause, recognizing that you're on the edge of emotional spending. You're trying to buy happiness with a new outfit. Instead, you close the email, slip into your walking shoes, and head outside for a breath of fresh air. By the time you're done with your walk, you're feeling better. The desire to buy the outfit has faded. After a few days, if you still find yourself thinking about the outfit and it fits within your budget, then you consider making the purchase.

Or maybe your best friend got the latest smartphone, and it's all they can talk about. You can't help but feel a twinge of envy. Your own phone suddenly seems old and out of date. The thought crosses your mind that maybe you should get a new smartphone, too.

You stop and think about this for a moment. Is this need for a new phone because yours isn't working, or is it because you're comparing what you have to your friend's? You realize your phone is working fine, and getting a new one would slow your progress toward reaching your financial goals. Instead, you decide to keep your current phone, reminding yourself that it's not a competition and that you have other priorities for your money.

Or, let's imagine you've walked into a store, intent on finding a birthday gift for your friend. As you pass the shoe section, a pair of stylish sandals catches your eye. You stop and pick them up, admiring their design. They're expensive, and you hadn't planned to buy anything for yourself, but you can already see how great they'd look with your favorite outfit.

You pause and feel the thrill of the impulse buy, but you remind yourself of the plan you've set. Instead of heading to the cash register, you take a photo of the sandals and move on. When you get home, you think about the sandals - do you really need another pair? Can you afford them without sacrificing your financial goals? If, after considering these questions, the sandals still seem like a worthwhile purchase, then you should consider buying them. But if they're out of your budget, you start looking for similar, more affordable options, or consider saving a little each month until you can afford them without straining your finances.

118

Here's an example of how one of my clients navigated this with her child in order to teach him how to make smart purchasing choices. It was a typical Saturday, and Lynn and her son, Max, were wrapping up their grocery shopping trip when Max spotted a toy store. They walked inside, and he was captivated by a pricey superhero action figure with an elaborate battle station. Lynn was tempted to buy it to please Max and share in his excitement. After all, he'd had a rough week at school that week. Maybe he deserved a special treat. She was on the cusp of emotional buying, motivated by the joy the toy would bring her son.

Then, Lynn recognized the importance of teaching Max about planning and making smart financial decisions. She explained to Max the need to stick to their plan. They would check their finances when they got home, and if they could afford the toy without affecting other needs, they could come back for it. If not, they could save a portion of Max's allowance each week until they could afford it. In managing the situation this way, Lynn not only avoided an impulse buy but also conveyed a valuable financial lesson to Max. It was a win-win for both of them.

Every story that I share offers a mirror, reflecting the choices we all face in our day-to-day lives. When we truly immerse ourselves in understanding our motivations, the power shifts. We become more in control of our finances rather than letting them control us. And within this empowered state, we're better positioned to sift through the noise, focusing on what genuinely resonates with our goals and values. The truth? It's more than just money; it's about honoring our personal journey, knowing that each decision either builds upon or detracts from the path we've envisioned.

Remember, life is filled with wants as much as needs. While we all deserve treats now and then, it's vital to ensure our desires come from a genuine place and not fleeting emotions.

Emotional buying, driven by how we feel in a moment, can sometimes divert us from our true financial path. Buying something is more than making a purchase; it's understanding our motivations behind each one. Every time that urge to buy emerges, pause and reflect on its true purpose in your life. With intention and careful consideration, you'll find that balance – letting you enjoy the pleasures of today without sacrificing the dreams of tomorrow.

What strategies are you going to use to help conquer emotional buying?

_____

_____

_____

_____

_____

_____

_____

_____

_____

_____

_____

_____

_____

_____

I CAN USE

MY WEALTH TO

CREATE OPPORTUNITIES

FOR MYSELF

AND OTHERS.

CHAPTER 9

THE MAGIC OF KEEPING SCORE

O n a typical spring day in mid-April of 2018, my bank reached out with the annoying task of filling out what is called a Personal Financial Statement (or PFS), as they do every year around this time, as part of renewing my husband's business line of credit. When I sat down to complete it, I didn't know this was going to be a game-changer in my life. You see, the PFS actually calculates your net worth. When I finished completing it, I almost fell out of my chair. It was the first time I had hit $1M net worth.

I was in shock. I couldn't believe I was a millionaire! It wasn't something I aspired to be. I had been intentional about making smart money decisions and building my wealth through investing in mutual funds and rental properties, but it was never a goal I set out to accomplish. I didn't feel like a millionaire, but how does a millionaire feel? Who knew? Regardless, I was one, and my husband and I had done it all on our own. Neither of us came from money. My parents lived paycheck to paycheck, and when my husband and I were first married, so did we. After that day, I actually looked forward to filling out the PFS every year as I watched my net worth continue to grow.

Jump to four years later, and another surprise - our net worth was now $2M! Good financial decisions, the rising value of our homes, and a helping hand from the stock market got us there. We doubled our net worth in only four years! The average person doubles their net worth in 10 years. I don't share any of this to brag. I am sharing this to let you know that it's possible for you, too. Our income didn't double. It grew a little as I started recognizing my personal worth and gaining better clients, but I was still in the six-figure range. But as I always say, what you focus on grows, and I was laser-focused on growing my wealth. The clarity I received from annually tracking my net worth gave me the vision I needed to make targeted financial decisions that boosted my net worth. Whenever I had a financial decision to make, I asked myself, "Will this increase or decrease my net worth?" which led to this substantial growth.

There were a few other notable financial wins during those four years. I had been saving like crazy to put my kids through college. I chose to save for their college in a Roth IRA retirement account instead of a 529 plan because retirement accounts do not count against you in the pursuit of financial aid. This decision turned out to have even more benefits than I expected.

Not only did it not count against us when seeking financial aid, but it would also add to my retirement savings if I didn't need to use it for their college tuition, which is exactly what happened. Two of my children dropped out of college to start their careers, and my third child went away to college but decided to come home and commute to college instead after her first semester. So, the $90K college tuition year I mentioned earlier in the book that I was so concerned about never happened. The total payment turned out to be around $20K, and I was able to use my home equity line of credit to pay for all their college expenses. Even with this major win, I continued to save because I had been doing it already, and I knew I could continue doing so. I was watching my wealth grow exponentially and watching the numbers in my Roth IRA account get larger and larger, and as a result, my net worth was growing fast. This was motivating and exciting!

When I look back to 14 years ago, my net worth was $330K. Today, it's $2M. During those first interim years, with three kids and bills piling up, growth was slow. It took nearly a decade to reach the $1M mark. But here's the thing – *it grew.* I tracked it and watched it grow every year. Like the tortoise in that old fairy tale, slow and steady wins the race. I tracked my net worth year after year. It was an inspiration when it was going in the right direction and a pause button when it wasn't. I was careful about how I spent money. I put money into things that would grow and also into myself. You see, you are your most important investment. The more you invest in you, the more you're worth. In fact, currently, the only expense that's higher than my professional development is the cost of my team. I always aim to better myself, not only for me but for everyone in my life.

What is your net worth? Do you know it? Your net worth serves as a snapshot of your financial health. Think of it as a balance sheet for your personal finances. On one side, you've got your assets. This includes everything you own that has tangible value: cash in the bank, investments like stocks or mutual funds, retirement plans, real estate properties, or vehicles. These assets are the positive side of your financial story; they represent your wealth accumulation.

On the flip side, there are liabilities. These are your debts or what you owe to others: mortgages, car loans, student loans, credit card balances, and other personal debts. If assets are the positive side, think of liabilities as the negative side.

Your net worth is the result of subtracting these liabilities from your assets. In simpler terms, Net Worth = Total Assets - Total Liabilities (debt). If the outcome is positive, it indicates your current net worth. A negative net worth means your debts surpass your assets. Try not to put any guilt, shame, or judgment on this number. Remember, it's only a figure. Don't give it more power than it deserves. It's a starting point from which you can grow, learn, and improve. Determining your net worth isn't about measuring your worth as a person or comparing yourself to others. Instead, it's a tool to help you understand where you stand financially, giving you a clearer vision of where you want to go and how to get there.

It's important to know your net worth before you start making changes. You need to know where you're starting in order to figure out how best to grow. It is important to know your net worth before you create a strategy. And keeping track of your net worth will keep you motivated and inspired.

I have a special tool that calculates your net worth for you called the "Wealth Tracking Dashboard" in the book portal. This calculator helps you figure out your net worth, which will help you make smart choices to grow your money. Simply input your numbers, and it'll spit out your net worth.

Here is the QR code to take you to the book portal:

We'll also calculate your net worth together at the end of this chapter. Calculating your net worth helps you understand your finances better. It's crucial to keep track of it over time to see how you're doing and make smart decisions about your money. It's important to remember that there is no shame or judgment when it comes to where you are starting financially.

Everyone's financial journey is different, and we all start from different places. Whether your net worth is positive or negative, it's a starting point, not a reflection of your worth as a person. The key is to focus on taking positive steps to improve your financial situation, no matter where you are now. By tracking your net worth, setting goals, and making wise financial choices, you can gradually work towards a brighter financial future. Remember, it's never too late to start, and small steps in the right direction can lead to significant progress over time. Stay motivated, be kind to yourself, and keep moving forward on your financial journey.

**WEALTH IS
A SOURCE OF
PRIDE AND
ACCOMPLISHMENT,
AND I CAN FEEL GOOD
ABOUT ACHIEVING IT.**

Let me share two contrasting stories from women in my Financially Empowered Sisterhood group program that illuminate this sentiment further.

Jennah was apprehensive when she first began calculating her net worth. As she confronted her financial realities, feelings of guilt and shame washed over her. Her net worth was in the negative. I shared with her, "It's only a number. It doesn't mean anything about who you are." She agreed and became determined to let her current net worth be a starting point. Her strategy to grow her wealth started with a focus on eliminating debt.

On the other hand, Dina, when taking stock of her assets and liabilities, was pleasantly surprised and felt a sense of calm from the exercise. It turns out she had more than she realized when it came to her net worth. This made her feel secure and also motivated her to grow it even more. This motivation led her to make changes in her lifestyle by cutting back on some things, like overbuying groceries, that ended up getting thrown out.

In one of our group sessions, I strongly emphasized to everyone, including Jennah and Dina, that we shouldn't give this number undue power or let it define our self-worth. After all, it's just a number. Oftentimes, we give numbers such power over us without even realizing it. Take the emotion out of the number, and don't let it mean anything about you.

Both experiences drive home the point that our emotional responses to our financial situations are deeply personal. And yet, regardless of where they started, both Jennah and Dina made commendable progress. Because they had a clear picture of their current financial situation, they could make choices to improve it. They both focused on their financial education and began tracking how they were using their money and how it was working for and against them. It wasn't the number that mattered as much as the action they took in response to it.

Remember this: financial education and the choices you make are what truly count. By tracking your net worth, setting goals, and making informed financial choices, you can progressively work towards a brighter financial future. It's never too late to begin, and incremental steps in the right direction can result in substantial progress over time. Stay motivated, be compassionate to yourself, and persistently advance on your financial journey.

Now that you know what your net worth is, let's discuss ways to boost it. There are many pathways to building wealth and boosting your net worth, depending on your risk tolerance. Remember when we identified our Money Behavior Styles? Keep your persona and animal in mind (both your strengths and what you could work to improve!) as you consider these suggestions. The important thing to remember is following pointed, intentional, long-term wealth-building strategies that boost your net worth. Slow and steady always wins the race when increasing your net worth. But first, you have to get in the game!

Get In the Game

My path has been paved with lessons and unique strategies that have served me well at my risk tolerance level. The primary way I've built my wealth is by investing in mutual funds, in both retirement and non-retirement accounts.

For investing, I've always been a fan of the "set it and forget it" monthly strategy, which is called an automatic investment plan. Every month, a set amount of money is withdrawn from my bank account and transferred into my investment account like a bill on automatic payment. This strategy has worked wonders. I believe in letting my money work for me over time. This has significantly increased my net worth consistently over the years since I started investing. We'll get more specific as to how to start investing later in this book. I'll show you exactly how to start investing and have laid out easy steps for you to start on your own. I have guided many women through these exact steps, and they've found it exciting, simple, and easy to do on their own. These steps completely take away any fears they may have about investing.

It might surprise you to learn that I don't obsessively watch the stock market every day. In fact, most days, I don't even tune into the news. My husband, on the other hand, is always in the loop. For my own peace of mind, I try to shield myself from the constant barrage of negativity in the media. It's all too draining. Yet, my husband has a habit of updating me whenever the stock market takes a dive, which I do appreciate.

You might be curious about how I educated myself in order to master the stock market. You'll recall from the opening chapter that there was a time when our combined family income was only $24,000, and we had two tiny toddlers under three. That is when we were living so tight that we even qualified for the Earned Income Credit, a benefit meant for low-income families. This credit is designed to ease the financial burdens by giving a bit back during tax season. Now, qualifying for this made me feel all kinds of ways. First, it was like a label screaming, "You're broke!" Second, it felt like I was betraying my mom's warnings by relying solely on my husband's income. My husband had recently started building his own lawn care business. Yes, we saw growth, but the initial expenses of setting up a new venture had us strapped financially. I loved our life, but deep down, I knew we needed more to get out of this situation.

A dear friend of mine turned out to be our silver lining. She was employed at Vanguard, a mutual fund investment company, and mentioned they were on the hunt for evening shift workers. The cherry on top? They offered health benefits even for part-timers, and at the time, we were paying for that ourselves. Seeing the potential, I jumped on board, landing a role in client services and assisting folks with their mutual fund accounts. Funny enough, all I knew about investing at that point was what I had read in the Money magazine article. But, thanks to my friend, I had landed an opportunity that was about to turn out to be one of the best decisions of my life.

Here's where the magic happened. I had committed that my family would never depend on my income since I wasn't sure I wanted to work long-term at Vanguard. And even though it was tight, we managed to live on my husband's newly formed lawn care business income of $24,000, which was also slowly growing. I made a plan: my paycheck would first cover our health insurance contribution, and the rest would go straight into a Vanguard mutual fund account. Over time, that dream house wasn't as distant as I had once imagined. With every bit of determination I had, I funneled as much as I could into my Vanguard account. Before I knew it, within a few short years, I had saved up the $20K we needed for the down payment on a bigger home for our growing family.

So, what's all this got to do with boosting your net worth? Not a lot. But here's the golden nugget: your current situation isn't your destiny. The beauty of life is its capacity for change. You have the power to pivot, to reshape your future. And sometimes, we can make do with a lot less than we think and still come out smiling. I've lived that truth time and again, and trust me, it always turns out more than "okay."

Now, when there is a significant drop in the market, my eyes light up. To me, a declining market shouts, "Stocks are on Sale!" In March 2020, the Dow Jones Industrial Average experienced its worst single-day point drop ever, falling nearly 3,000 points. This drop was a result of most people panicking and hastily withdrawing their investments, causing the market to tumble. I saw it as an opportunity to invest even more and took a big risk.

At this time, when COVID first made its impact, I was in the process of pulling equity from my primary residence and one of my rental properties. I had plans to invest in a new property in sunny Florida. But as luck would have it, a day after I finalized the refinance paperwork, the nation came to a screeching halt. Flights to Florida were grounded, and I was left with $200K idly sitting in my bank account while my mortgage refinance was accruing interest, and I had no immediate investment plan.

Rather than despair, I decided to dance with fate. Taking a bold step, I funneled the entire $200K into a Vanguard mutual fund. I won't lie; my heart raced a tad faster during that time. While other people were exiting the stock market because of COVID fears, as shown in the graph below, I invested, and to my delight, my leap of faith reaped a windfall. I profited $22K in a mere six weeks! Such returns were beyond my expectations. This windfall even allowed me to buy a bigger condo in Florida than the one I'd originally intended to purchase. But let me be clear – while I triumphed this time, this was a risky move. My years of market observations have taught me that such severe disruptions, like the one caused by COVID, tend to be short-lived.

If you look at this graph, you'll see a comforting trend: the market always rises again. If you'd held onto your investments during dips, your net worth would've remained intact. This was true for me during the dip of the COVID-19 pandemic. In the coming months, the market rebounded. Yet, a common pitfall many struggle to avoid is withdrawing their money during these lows and reinvesting during the highs – a surefire strategy to minimize growth. My experience has taught me that with a horizon of at least five years, patience and persistence can weather any market storm. When you take a look at this chart, it's like a roadmap showing the power of sticking to your financial game plan.

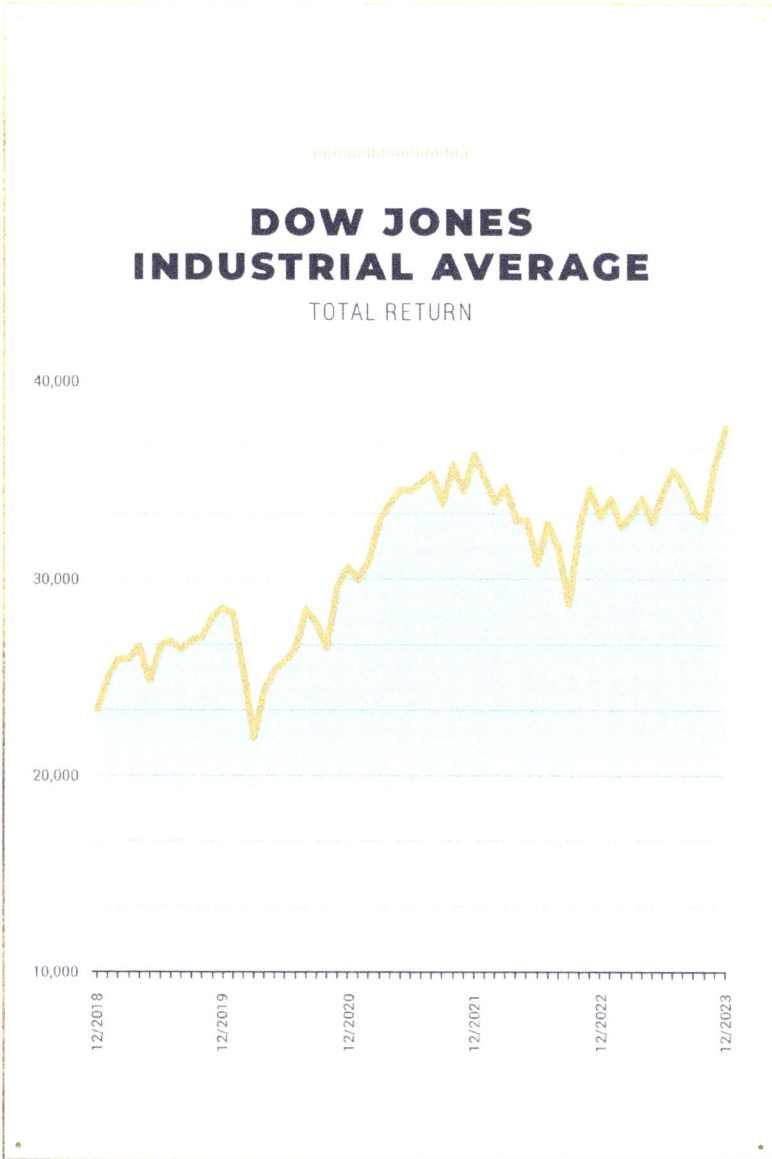

DOW JONES INDUSTRIAL AVERAGE
TOTAL RETURN

Building your net worth can feel a lot like a game of Monopoly. In Monopoly, everyone begins with a certain amount of money, like when we initially start saving or investing. As the game progresses, you make strategic decisions like buying or trading properties. This mirrors real-life decisions we make on how to best use our money to increase our net worth.

Rolling the dice in Monopoly adds an element of surprise, as you can't predict where you'll land next. This is similar to how life throws us unexpected events that can affect our net worth. Sometimes, these surprises can boost our net worth, like receiving unexpected money or rewards. But at other times, unexpected expenses might crop up, potentially reducing our net worth.

In Monopoly, passing 'Go' is a moment of victory, and it's just as rewarding when we reach our financial milestones in real life, like hitting a savings goal or watching our net worth reach a new high. The process of growing our net worth can feel like a strategic, fun game. It requires thoughtful planning, wise decisions, and a little bit of luck. The more we play, the better we get, and the more enjoyable the game becomes.

Prompt: Calculate your Net Worth

1. List the assets you own and how much they're worth. List all the things you own that are valuable. This includes money you have, like cash or savings accounts. Don't forget to include any investments you have, like stocks or bonds and retirement accounts. If you have a house or a car, write that down, too. Estimate the value of each item by looking at your bank statements or doing some research online. You can check Zillow for home values and Kelly Blue Book for car values. Add up the values to find out how much you own.

Make your list here:

2. List what you owe and how much. This could be loans you took out, like for a home, a car, or education, or credit card debt (revolving only). Write down the exact amount you owe for each thing. You can find this information on your loan statements or by calling the companies you owe money to. Add up all the amounts to see how much you owe in total. Don't forget any personal loans you may owe.

Make your list here:

---

3. To find your net worth, subtract the total amount you owe from the total value of what you own. This number is your net worth. If the result is positive, it means you own more than you owe. That's a good thing! If the result is negative, it means you owe more than you own. This gives you an idea of your financial situation. Remember, your net worth can change over time as you save money or pay off debts.

Do the math here:

TOTAL ASSETS: _____

SUBTRACT TOTAL DEBT: _____

NET WORTH:_____

TODAY'S DATE: _____

**RICH PEOPLE
ARE HARDWORKING
AND DEDICATED
INDIVIDUALS
WHO HAVE
EARNED THEIR SUCCESS.**

CHAPTER 10

THE 7% RULE AND OTHER FINANCIAL GAME-CHANGERS

There are many ways you can optimize your finances. In this chapter, I'm going to share three specific strategies that have brought me and my clients the most success. The first way is using debt wisely and becoming debt savvy. Contrary to what a lot of financial experts say, being debt-free can actually keep you from optimizing your wealth. The second strategy is saving in a Roth IRA. The flexibility in saving in this IRA is amazing, and it also grows tax-free. The third is financially educating yourself through books, podcasts, courses, or a mentor or coach. For legal reasons, I'll reiterate my disclaimer: The following is for informational purposes only and should not be considered as financial advice. Always consult with a financial advisor before making any investment decisions. But trust me, this information has had lasting impacts on my financial success as well as the success of my clients. Let's dive in!

Strategy 1: Being Debt Savvy

During my college years, my finance professor enlightened us about the dynamics of inflation and interest rates. In one class, he shared a perspective that really got me thinking. He mentioned that in an environment where inflation reduces the buying power of your dollar by about 3% each year, a loan with an interest rate of 3% or less could essentially be considered "free money." This bit of wisdom truly stuck with me and influenced how I approach debt. For instance, when buying a car, if the financing interest rate was less than 3%, I'd avoid putting any money down, saving that money for other uses or investments instead. This way, instead of tying up my funds in the car, I could use them in other ways that could generate more wealth in the long run, like putting that additional cash in a mutual fund.

Here's where my **7% Rule** comes into play, a strategy I've personally benefited from and share with my coaching clients. It simply means this: if your debt comes with an interest rate higher than 7%, you should prioritize paying it off quickly. However, for debts with interest rates below 7%, stick to regular payments and consider investing the additional money in a mutual fund. Let's dive a bit deeper to show you why this approach can be more advantageous.

Imagine you've just bought a home with a 30-year mortgage of $250,000 at an interest rate of 5%. You might hear advice suggesting paying an extra $100 per month to clear the mortgage faster. This scenario would save you around $38K in interest charges. Many experts categorize all debt as bad debt. However, what I propose is a potentially more prosperous path. By investing that $100 monthly into a mutual fund, unsteady of your mortgage, that averages a 10% annual return (a figure based on the data cited in a 2021 Morningstar article, which you can find on the book portal,) at the end of your mortgage term, you could have approximately $215K in your mutual fund account, a sum substantially larger than the interest saved by paying the mortgage early. Understand that this is a long-term gain. If your loan doesn't have at least 5-7 years left on it, it might not be the best option for you. You should weigh all your options and scenarios carefully.

If you want to play around with different scenarios on your own mortgage, student loan, or other loans, I've created an easy-to-use free calculator called the "Wealth Winning Calculator."

You can find it in the book portal. Every time I show my coaching clients and do this experiment, their minds are blown.

When it comes to optimizing your finances and being debt-free, you might find one financial expert's name popping up frequently - Dave Ramsey. He is a well-known advocate of the "debt-free" model. I have a considerable degree of respect for Dave. In fact, I undertook his financial coaching certification course, which was an interesting and educational experience.

One of the more memorable "success stories" from Ramsey's course involved a couple who chose to sell their house to embrace the "debt-free" lifestyle, only to end up renting, which is essentially paying off someone else's mortgage and building their wealth. That approach didn't quite resonate with my financial strategy. While this couple was "debt-free," I didn't think that building someone else's wealth through paying rent was the best financial scenario.

My financial approach doesn't follow Ramsey's model because the "debt-free" model is, in my opinion, not the best way to build wealth quickly. My personal journey towards creating wealth - which has led me to a multiple seven-figure net worth- was down a different path, a path that I firmly believe holds potential for others to build a high net worth exponentially quicker than the debt-free model. Instead, I utilized the 7% rule when it came to debt and invested in mutual funds and rental properties with all the additional money I could.

Owning a home without a mortgage, as is recommended in a "debt-free" strategy, is often out of reach for most people. In addition, if you strictly follow a "debt-free" strategy, your credit score becomes nonexistent - the score you need to secure a mortgage. In my experience, it's important to note that not all debt is bad, especially if it's low interest. It can seem like free money, if handled correctly.

I made my wealth by using debt wisely. I only put 20% of my own money into my house, as well as any rental property I bought, because the mortgage rates were less than 7%. The rest of the money I used was borrowed. I continued to invest the rest of my money in mutual funds to continue to grow my net worth, which was my primary goal. Remember,

I was able to grow my net worth from $350K in 2009 to over $2 million in 2023. I saw a 500% growth in only 14 years from using this strategy. It goes to show that if used correctly, debt can become a helpful tool on your path to prosperity.

Making sure you have a good credit score is also important so you can get the best interest rates on your loans to grow your wealth this way. I suggest checking your credit score and pulling your credit report once per year. The credit report will give you a list of all the accounts on your open credit accounts. Always review it for accuracy. This report will not give you your credit score, but often, you can get that on your credit card statement or an online portal. As of this writing, Capital One, Bank of America, American Express, Chase, and Discover, to name a few, have this information available either online, in their app, or on your statements.

Once you know your credit score, here are ten techniques you can use to improve it:

1. Pay Your Bills on Time: Late or missed payments can have a significant negative impact on your credit score. Make sure you're paying all your bills on time, including utilities, rent, and any loans you have. Setting up automatic payments is a great way to make sure you are not late on any bills or payments.
2. Reduce Your Credit Card Debt: High levels of credit card debt can lower your credit score. Focus on reducing your credit card debt or other high-interest debt. It is always optimal to try to pay your credit cards off in full every month.
3. Keep Your Credit Utilization Low: Your credit utilization ratio is the amount of your available credit that you're using. It's generally recommended to keep this ratio below 30%. For example, if you have a credit card with a $10,000 limit, try to keep your balance below $3,000.
4. Don't Close Old Credit Accounts: The length of your credit history can affect your credit score. Even if you're not using a credit card, as long as it's not costing you in annual fees, keeping it open can help your credit score. This helps in several ways. The length or amount of time you've had a credit card increases your score and adds to your overall amount of credit available and utilization. If you don't want to use a card anymore, place it in a drawer somewhere, but don't close the account.
5. Apply for Credit Sparingly: Every time you apply for credit, it results in a hard inquiry on your credit report, which can lower your score. Try to apply for new credit only when necessary.

6. Dispute Any Inaccuracies: If you notice any errors on your credit report, be sure to dispute them with the credit bureau. This can involve a bit of paperwork, but removing erroneous negative information can improve your score.

7. Establish a Diverse Credit Mix: Creditors like to see that you can handle different types of credit responsibly. If it makes sense for your situation, having a mix of installment loans (like a car loan or mortgage) and revolving credit (like credit cards) can improve your score.

8. Become an Authorized User: If a close friend or family member has a strong credit history, they might be willing to add you as an authorized user on their credit card. This can help boost your credit score, as their payment history can then contribute positively to your own credit report. This is also a great way to help your children establish credit at an early age.

9. Avoid Maxing Out Credit Cards: Even if you're paying off your balance each month, running up high balances can hurt your score. Try to keep your balance as low as possible throughout the billing cycle to keep your credit utilization ratio low.

10. Increase Your Credit Limit: This may seem counterintuitive, but increasing your credit limit can lower your credit utilization ratio, provided you don't increase your spending along with it. This can be done either by requesting a credit limit increase from your credit card issuer or by opening a new credit card and spreading your charges between the cards. I like to use different credit cards for different purposes. I have a credit card for every rental property I have. I would then take a label maker and put a label on which card was for which property, which card was for personal use, which card was for business use, and so on. The individual credit cards made it so easy to track everything. This allowed me to know exactly which expenses were personal and which expenses were with which property or business. Also, making tax time a breeze.

It is also important to protect your credit score and your credit. Unfortunately, we live in a world where stealing someone's identity is all too common. Protecting your credit will save lots of aggravation and stress in the future. There are a few different credit monitoring and credit protecting services out there, but I personally use Identity Guard and have found it useful to create peace of mind.

Other than feeling secure that my credit is protected, using Identity Guard also came in handy one time when I was buying a new car, and the finance manager ran my credit over a dozen times. As I said above, every time someone runs your credit, it lowers your credit score. One finance manager at a local car dealership went crazy and submitted my financial information to over a dozen different banks for a car loan application I submitted. I received an email from Identity Guard every time one of these banks ran my credit. As you can imagine, I was angry with the finance manager for not reaching out to me before he did this and asking my permission.

These emails allowed me to immediately call the dealership and put a stop to it. I not so pleasantly schooled the finance manager why what he was doing was a problem. However, I would have never known this was happening if it wasn't for Identity Guard emails flowing in one after another.

Another benefit to having a good credit score is if you have a big purchase or investment you want to make, you can get a 0% introductory interest rate on a new credit card. Oftentimes, I'll open a new credit card with a 0% interest rate for 12 months when I am going to make a big purchase. One of my favorite investments is in professional development and coaches. Doing this has shown tremendous results in my business. Coaches have drastically helped me get where I am today. Usually, they will give a "pay in full" discount or a monthly pay option. If the pay-in-full discount is over 7% (i.e., the 7% rule), and it almost always is, I open a new credit card and take the pay-in-full discount then stagger the payments over the 12-month period or however long the program is interest-free. I've saved thousands of dollars making payments this way. In fact, while crafting this book, I chose to work with a writing coach and paid for that education in exactly this way.

Now, let's discuss debt through the eyes of one of my clients, Morgan. Morgan is in her late twenties and is very driven. She has a marketing business and also has a multi-level marketing (MLM) product-based business. When I posed the question to Morgan about her biggest takeaway from our sessions together, she got excited about several things, but changing her attitude around debt was her biggest "aha" moment. "I remember it vividly," she said. "You introduced this paradigm-shifting revelation that 'debt isn't necessarily bad,' and it transformed my entire outlook on personal finance."

Morgan's story is common. Fresh out of college, she was thrown into a world for which she was unprepared. Her parents, influenced by their own priorities and connections, had chosen her college for her and agreed to pay for it. And while she had been grateful for their initial support, unforeseen circumstances led to an abrupt change in their financial involvement. She started telling me this story by sharing, "They had initially agreed to handle the tuition. Yet, by the end of my journey, they'd divorced and decided that they no longer wanted any connection to my student loans. Suddenly, I was staring at a debt north of $100,000." I could hear the shock in her voice when she first told me about this experience.

She went on to say, "This amount of debt was overwhelming, especially for someone fresh out of college." With no guidance and the emotional toll of the debt weighing heavily on her, she impulsively used her lifelong savings to pay off a significant chunk of her student loans. She shared with me her biggest takeaway from FES, "When you highlighted the concept of debt during our meeting, I was in complete shock." Then she said, "I remember scribbling down notes, thinking about how I perceive debt so differently." She continued with excitement, "The most transformative idea that I've taken away, one that will significantly shape my decisions moving forward, is the principle of the 7% Rule." She went on to say, "It's wiser not to rush into paying off debt." I knew her mindset was transformed and she was heading down the right path to prosperity when she added, "Also, by spacing out payments, you're building your credit score, which is ultimately to your advantage. I had never thought of it that way. Having this new perspective, this deeper understanding, opened up so many possibilities for me. Now, I see that I don't need vast sums to make impactful financial moves. Even an extra $100 or $50 a month can make a difference when invested wisely. This realization was truly groundbreaking for me. It reshaped how I viewed my financial future." I was such a proud coach!

Morgan's story is a great example of how when debt is understood and managed correctly, it can be a tool rather than a chain. It was exciting for me to see her embrace this new knowledge and stride confidently towards building her wealth. Morgan has a great future ahead of her to start building her wealth.

Being debt savvy is one of the most important wealth-building strategies you can implement. It's more about seeing debt as a tool, just as money is a tool, to get started building your wealth. The next tool we will discuss is around saving. Without saving, it's hard to build your wealth and create a path to prosperity.

WEALTH IS A SIGN OF ABUNDANCE AND PROSPERITY, AND I CAN ATTRACT IT INTO MY LIFE.

Strategy 2: Saving in Roth IRAs

Another way to optimize your finances is through savings in a Roth Individual Retirement Account, known as a Roth IRA. It is a savvy way to tuck money away for your retirement and other life events. Let's dive into why this is such a smart move. The most valuable thing about Roth IRAs is that you pay taxes on the money before you put it into a Roth IRA and not when you retire, as with other traditional IRAs. As Roth IRAs grow, the returns are never taxed as long as you wait to use them until your retirement age. When you're ready to kick back and enjoy your golden years, every penny you withdraw, along with all the earnings from your investments, is yours to use tax-free. This can lead to substantial tax savings in the long run.

One of the standout features of a Roth IRA is the unparalleled flexibility it offers. With this retirement account, your money is easily accessible. And also, unlike other retirement savings options, there's no specific age at which you're required to start making withdrawals. This allows your savings to continue to grow, potentially leading to a more prosperous retirement.

What if you need cash quickly? Another advantage of the Roth IRA shines here. You're allowed to access the money you've put in, your contributions, without incurring any penalties or owing income taxes. You can only access the contributions, not the returns on your money. This sets the Roth IRA apart from many other retirement plans, which often impose substantial penalties for early withdrawals. Whether you're planning for the long haul or you end up needing funds in a pinch, a Roth IRA provides valuable flexibility and access to your savings.

An often-overlooked benefit of a Roth IRA is that it can be a smart way to save for your child's college education. When the time comes to complete those financial aid forms, the money stashed away in your Roth IRA isn't considered an asset. This means it won't impact your child's eligibility for financial aid, possibly making more resources available to them for their education.

But what happens if they don't need all of it for college? Roth IRAs shine here as well. Any funds that aren't used for education can remain in the account, continuing to grow tax-free for your retirement. Therefore, a Roth IRA provides a dual-purpose savings approach, ready to support your child's education expenses or to secure your future retirement—whichever way the road turns.

Lastly, a Roth IRA is also a wonderful tool for passing wealth to your loved ones. If you leave the money in your Roth IRA to your kids or grandkids, they won't owe any income tax when they withdraw it. And remember, a Roth IRA gives you lots of investment options, like stocks, bonds, and mutual funds, to help grow your savings.

Of course, Roth IRAs have rules about who can contribute and how much you can put in each year. Additionally, you won't get a tax deduction for the money you contribute now, like you do with some other retirement accounts. But in the grand scheme of things, these can be small trade-offs for the benefits of a Roth IRA.

The Roth IRA income and contribution rules change every year, so be sure to look up the most current numbers before you start. In 2023, the contribution limits were $6,500 or $7,500 if you're 50-plus. The Roth IRA income limits for 2023 were less than $153,000 for single tax filers and less than $228,000 for those married filing jointly. A quick Google search should be able to give you the most up-to-date information.

Saving in a Roth IRA, if eligible, is one of the best-kept secrets I discovered for growing my wealth. I learned this and many other strategies by continuing to educate myself and thinking of different ways to maximize my wealth. This is why I highly recommend this third strategy—perhaps most of all.

Strategy 3: Financially Educating Yourself

Finally, financially educating yourself is truly the best way you can optimize your finances. Staying informed about financial trends, strategies, and tools can help you make better decisions about your money and help you learn things you might not have known. Sometimes, we don't know what we don't know.

Here are four ways to improve your financial education:

1. Books, especially audiobooks, offer an accessible and efficient avenue to expand your understanding of wealth creation, money management, and financial manifestation. Incorporating audiobooks into daily activities like walking, whether you're solo or accompanied by your furry friends, allows you to learn while also taking care of your physical well-being - a satisfying blend of mind and body engagement.

2. Courses and webinars are a valuable avenue for expanding your financial knowledge. Platforms like Udemy offer an extensive selection of affordable courses, often priced under $20, providing an economical way to go deeper into

financial topics. Beyond the affordability, the beauty of these digital courses lies in their flexibility—you can learn at your own pace and on your own time. In addition, many financial coaches and experts like myself provide free webinars or masterclasses that are treasure troves of financial wisdom. By attending such classes, you can gain insights directly from professionals and even get the opportunity to ask questions. I frequently host different masterclasses, always updating and enriching the content.

To be alerted to my next free masterclass, simply sign up here

1. Podcasts are an incredibly handy tool for building financial literacy. They're an easily accessible and free way to learn on the go or while multitasking. The vast array of financial podcasts available caters to all interests, from personal finance to investment strategies. Their conversational style makes complex topics more digestible. Plus, hearing real-life stories can offer insightful lessons and motivation. In essence, podcasts offer a flexible, engaging way to enhance your financial knowledge.

2. Consider hiring a financial coach. A good coach can be beneficial when you're trying to learn more about managing your money. It's like having a guide on your side, helping you navigate the twists and turns of finances, both in your personal life and for your business. A financial coach provides advice that matches your personal goals, offering real and practical steps. This guidance can be a game-changer in dealing with money matters and making the most of opportunities. One of the biggest benefits of a financial coach is learning to make smart money choices, managing potential risks, and building wealth. Plus, it's important to remember that everyone starts from a different place in their money journey. A good financial coach shouldn't judge or blame you for past decisions but rather focus on helping you improve from where you are now. Working with a financial coach isn't only about getting advice; it's about making the path to financial well-being clearer and more achievable, and most of all, it's about gaining an education on making the best decisions for your financial future.

One of the most profitable nuggets of information came from a book I read (well, listened to), *Rich Dad Poor Dad* by Robert Kiyosaki. Although I didn't resonate with everything he discussed, there was this one gem that proved priceless – well, not priceless, because I know the price. It saved me $80,000 in taxes! I was on my way back from dropping a friend off at the airport who was visiting me at my Florida home. As I often do when I'm by myself in the car, I started listening to an audiobook. Kiyosaki said you can roll over your gain from a rental property to buy another rental property through what is called a 1031 Exchange. At this point, we knew we wanted to upgrade our Florida home from a condo to a single-family home, but we intended to wait until my husband retired. What Kiyosaki said made it clear that I could sell both my properties now, roll it into a new rental property in Florida, and not pay any capital gains tax. Then, I could convert it into a home for us a few years later when my husband retired.

Excited, I immediately reached out to my CPA. He not only confirmed Kiyosaki's advice but also sent over resources so I could dive deeper. My realtor, too, echoed this sentiment and connected me to a specialized service that would handle the 1031 Exchange. Thanks to this newfound knowledge, I sidestepped what would've been an $80,000 tax hit.

Now, take a moment and imagine this: What if, like me, you stumbled upon a life-altering financial insight from a simple book, podcast, or course? Now, elevate that thought. Imagine the knowledge you could unlock and apply with guidance from an experienced and savvy financial coach. The possibilities are endless, and the rewards can be huge.

Remember, never underestimate the power of education and continuous learning. It's the way to light your path to financial prosperity. Always be curious, always be ready to learn, and always believe that your next big financial breakthrough could be right around the corner. The journey to financial independence is filled with surprises, and armed with knowledge, you'll be ready to embrace them all.

Prompt: Do a little research. List at least six books, podcasts, or courses that you think could improve your financial education. And yes, this book can count as one!

WEALTH

IS A RESOURCE

THAT CAN BE USED

TO CREATE

MEANINGFUL IMPACT

AND POSITIVE CHANGE

IN THE WORLD.

CHAPTER 11

CONQUER THE MARKET

I'm sure you've heard the saying, "When one door closes, another one opens." I came across a popular free webinar online aimed at helping women navigate the investment world. I wanted to see what they were doing, so I signed up. While the focus of this particular webinar was more on mindset tools than actual investing strategies, it made me realize something. Shaping our mindset is an important step in any journey, including investing.

It did make me wonder, however, about how powerful it would be if someone could offer a step-by-step guide to not only empower your money mindset but also offer practical advice and tools on how to get your feet wet in the world of investing. That's where this chapter comes in.

In full disclosure, I am not an "investment advisor," but my experiences have sculpted me into someone who can provide you with a solid starting point to do it on your own. I've discovered that you can independently grow your wealth, even without an investment advisor. And you are always going to have your best interests in mind. Of course, seeking professional guidance is always an option, but I believe in the potential that lies within each of us to take charge of our financial health and wealth to create a path to prosperity.

As you may remember, my own investment journey began with an article from a Money magazine article and a monthly investment of $50 – which, in today's world, would cover a simple dinner out. It was a leap of faith I took without any knowledge or guidance. And if I could do it, so can you. But I am also going to help and empower you with a lot more knowledge than I had to get started investing today in this chapter.

Navigating the stock market and mutual funds might seem scary, but with the right insights, it becomes a simple and exciting journey of financial empowerment. Remember the enlightening graph from a previous chapter? Let's take a look at it again.

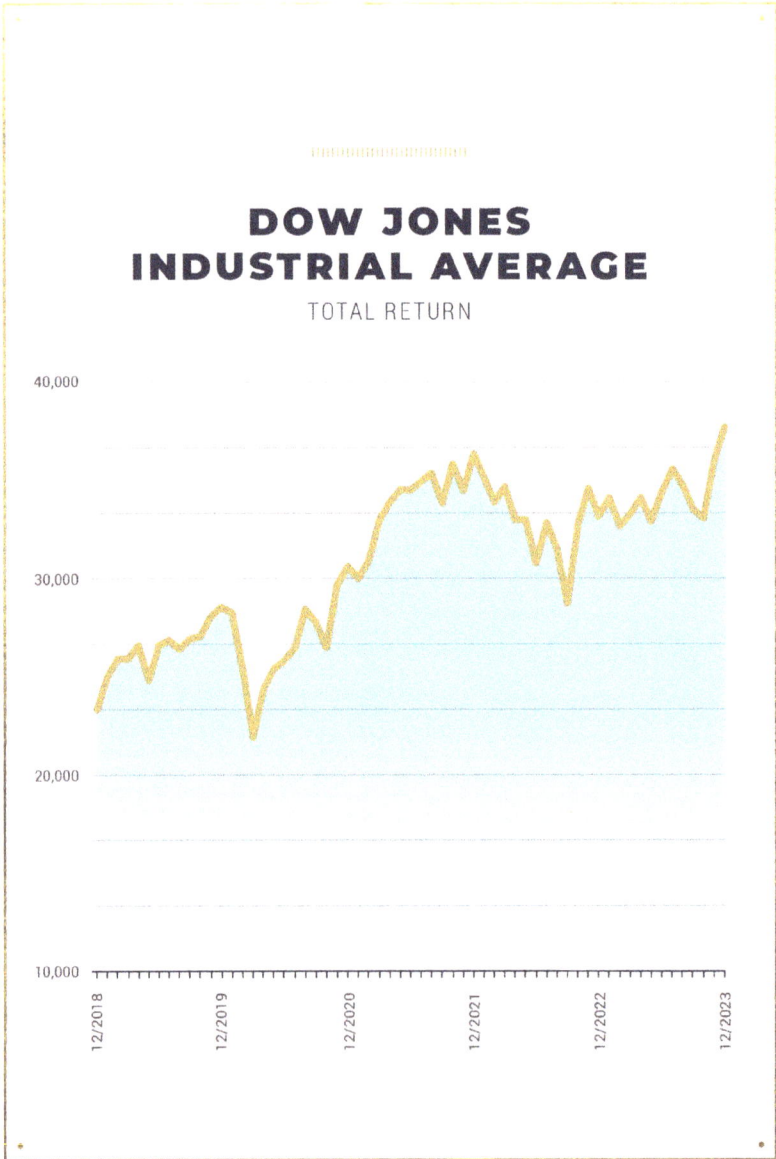

DOW JONES INDUSTRIAL AVERAGE

TOTAL RETURN

Why am I showing you this again? Because pretty much all mutual funds, if invested in US stocks, will follow this trajectory of the stock market. So here is a secret that investment advisors don't want you to know – it's pretty hard to pick the wrong mutual funds. Mutual funds follow the stock market as a whole and fluctuate in the same way for the most part. Yes, nearly all of them. This is why you can invest on your own, and you'll probably do comparably as well as you would have if you used a financial advisor— and it won't cost you any fees. You won't have to worry whether or not this person has your best interests at heart, and you'll feel so empowered making your own decisions and tracking your growing wealth.

Let's back up for a second. Are you wondering, "What even *is* a mutual fund?" A mutual fund is an investment vehicle designed to provide broad exposure to the stock market. It's like a big collection or a "basket" of different stocks, managed by an investment professional known as a fund manager who is trained to pick the best stocks for the fund. That's their job.

When you invest in a mutual fund, instead of having to choose individual stocks (which can be risky and require lots of time and knowledge), you are putting your money into this collection of stocks. The fund manager takes care of all the challenging parts for you, including researching, buying, selling, and tracking the stocks within the fund to get you the best return on your money.

Like stocks, mutual funds also have shares. When you invest your money in a mutual fund, you're essentially buying shares or portions of the fund. Each share represents a part of the fund's holdings. The price of each mutual fund share is determined by the net asset value (NAV), which is the total value of all the assets in the fund (all the stocks it holds) minus any liabilities, divided by the total number of shares. Your money is pooled together with other investors to form the total value of the mutual fund. This pool of money is used to buy shares in a variety of different companies. When you buy shares, you're buying a slice of this entire collection of stocks, proportional to the amount of money you've invested. As the price of a single stock rises and falls, the NAV of a mutual fund share changes daily as the total value of the assets in the fund increases or decreases. It's through buying and selling these shares at different NAVs that investors can make or lose money in mutual funds.

The primary advantage of mutual funds is diversification. Because they invest in a variety of different stocks, the risk is spread out. If one stock performs poorly, it might be offset by another stock that's performing well. Investing in a mutual fund is generally less risky than investing in individual stocks because of this diversification. If you put all your money in a single company's stock, like Enron, for example, and the company fails, you could lose all of your investment. But if you invest in a mutual fund that includes hundreds of different companies, the poor performance or failure of a single company, even one as big as Enron, won't have as severe an impact. The losses from one company are diluted by the gains from others, spreading out and thereby reducing your risk. Thus, mutual funds provide a safety net that individual stock investments lack.

Mutual funds come in various targets, each offering a different mix of stocks and a different investment focus. For example, "large cap" funds invest in big, established companies that are often household names that you'd know of. They might not grow as fast as smaller companies, but they're generally seen as more stable. On the other hand, "small-cap" and "mid-cap" funds invest in smaller and medium-sized companies that have more growth potential but also carry more risk. Then we have "international" or "global" funds, which invest in companies located outside of the US, adding geographical diversity and a little more risk.

"Sector" funds focus on specific industries like technology, healthcare, or finance and are also a bit riskier. Finally, "index" funds aim to mirror the performance of a specific market index, like the S&P 500, by buying all (or a sample) of the stocks in that index. Each of these fund types carries its own risk and return characteristics, and they can all play a unique role in your investment strategy.

Now that you're equipped with a fundamental understanding of what a mutual fund is, you're well on your way to start your investing journey. The broad exposure to the market that mutual funds provide, coupled with professional management and diversification benefits, makes them a go-to choice for many investors.

It's exciting, isn't it? The thought of your money working for you, potentially growing with the ups and downs of various companies included in your chosen fund, is thrilling. You're not a spectator watching from the sidelines; you're right there in the action, participating in the financial markets. Ready to take that first step? Here's a guide to walk you through the process of investing in funds. Let's dive in!

Step 1: Pick a mutual fund company. Research a mutual fund company in which you want to invest. Some companies have a minimum investment requirement, and some do not. What I did was start with a company that did not, then once I grew my investment to the minimum amount that was required to invest in a different one that I liked, I moved it. Here are a few companies that you might consider:

1. Vanguard: Vanguard is known for its low-cost index funds and typically has a low initial investment requirement, often around $3,000 or even less, for its Exchange-Traded Funds (ETFs). ETFs are investment funds that are traded on stock exchanges, similar to individual stocks, but they are actually mutual funds. They are designed to track the performance of a specific mutual fund with a lower investment requirement. You can typically open an ETF for as little as $1.

2. Fidelity Investments: Fidelity offers a wide range of mutual funds and has lowered its initial investment requirements in recent years. Some funds have minimum initial investments as low as $1.

3. Schwab: Charles Schwab provides access to a variety of mutual funds and offers low-cost investment options. The company has reduced its initial investment requirements, and some funds may have minimums as low as $1.

4. T. Rowe Price: T. Rowe Price offers a selection of mutual funds and has varying minimum initial investment requirements. Some funds may have minimums in the range of $1,000 to $2,500, while others may be as low as $100.

5. American Funds: American Funds offers a range of mutual funds, and the initial investment requirements vary depending on the fund. Many of their funds have minimum initial investments between $250 and $1,000.

6. TD Ameritrade: TD Ameritrade provides access to a wide selection of mutual funds from different fund companies. While the initial investment requirements may vary based on the specific funds, some options have low minimums starting around $100.

Step 2: Pick a fund. This is the step that most people are afraid of. But as I mentioned, it's really hard to pick the wrong fund. But to make it easier, I'll show you exactly what to look at. You'll want to find the list of performance for all the mutual funds in the company you choose. You'll know you're at the right place when you see a list that has percentages for YTD, 1-year, 5-year, and 10-year returns for the mutual funds. I want you to look at the 5-year return column. This is your key marker. Why not the 1 year or YTD? First, investing is for long-term savings. And second, the YTD and 1 year are often skewed. If the fund is having a great year, these numbers will be high. But what that means is they are destined to go down, not up. And you may start investing and expect this rate to continue, but it won't. Looking at the 5-year column is more realistic of what the fund will do. Actually, if the 5-year is much higher than the 1-year, then the fund will have the potential to go up, and that would be a good time to invest in it. Most importantly, find a fund that has a good 5-year rate of return and go for it. You'll also notice that most of the 5-year returns don't vary as much as the 1-year. They may also have a rating of risk on each fund. If you are saving for the long term, such as retirement, then you can try a riskier fund. However, if it's going to keep you up at night if it goes down, start with a less risky investment.

Step 3: Invest! At this point, all you need to do is follow the steps, open an account, and start investing. I also suggest using an automatic investment plan (AIP). This way, you can set it and forget it, and it will be like a bill that comes out of your bank account every month. That will be your first step into making passive income through investing and growing your wealth.

Another great thing about using an AIP strategy is something they call "dollar cost averaging." Think of it like this: you put the same amount of money into a mutual fund on a regular schedule, either every week or every month, no matter if the price is high or low. So, when the price is down, that same amount gets you more shares, and when it's up, you get fewer shares. Over time, this can average out the cost of each share you buy. The best part? You don't have to stress about the perfect time to invest. Keep putting your money in, and you'll ride out the market's ups and downs. It's a steady and consistent approach that's worked well for me and many others when investing in mutual funds.

When investing in stock mutual funds, it's crucial to be aware of the various fees involved, as they can significantly impact your returns over time. These costs come in several forms. The most common is the "expense ratio," which is an annual fee that all funds charge their shareholders. This covers fund management, administrative expenses, and other operational costs. Then there are "load" fees, which are sales charges you pay when you buy (front-end load) or sell (back-end load) shares in the fund. Some funds may charge a "redemption fee" if you sell your shares within a certain period, typically a few months to a year from the purchase date.

After learning about these various fees, you might be wondering if there are mutual funds out there that help you keep some of these costs down. The good news is: Yes, there are! Several well-known mutual fund companies offer "no-load" funds, meaning you won't be charged for buying or selling shares. These include Vanguard, renowned for its low-cost index funds; Fidelity Investments, which offers a broad selection of no-load funds covering various sectors;

T. Rowe Price, known for its diverse offering of no-load funds; and Charles Schwab, a reputable brokerage that also provides an array of no-load mutual funds. However, remember that while these funds don't have load fees, they may still have other costs, such as expense ratios, which cover the costs of managing the fund. Always take a look or ask questions about any fees when choosing your investments.

I CAN

ADMIRE AND APPRECIATE

WEALTHY PEOPLE

FOR THEIR

ACCOMPLISHMENTS

AND CONTRIBUTIONS

TO SOCIETY.

Keep in mind that investment advisors, while providing valuable advice and management services, also charge for their expertise. These fees usually come in two forms: fixed fees and percentage-based fees. The second is a certain percentage of the assets the advisor manages for you, typically ranging from 0.5% to 2% per year. Some advisors may also earn commissions on the products they sell to you.

But here's a piece of good news: if you're comfortable taking on the responsibility, you can choose to invest in mutual funds on your own and eliminate the fees charged by investment advisors. This approach can save you a significant amount of money over time, allowing it to remain invested and grow even more. Managing your own investments requires some initial research and selecting your own fund or funds, monitoring your portfolio occasionally, and making adjustments if you think it's necessary. But also remember that investing is long-term, and making adjustments too often can hurt your performance.

Over and over, in my own investments and watching the investments of clients, I see that one of the toughest things to handle when you're investing on your own is fear. The thought of making a wrong choice or watching the value go down can be scary. This fear can discourage many from even starting to invest or cause them to make hasty decisions when the market drops. But it's important to remember, though it's normal to feel scared, fear doesn't help when you're investing. Slow and steady wins the race of investing and growing your wealth.

Let's take a hypothetical scenario as an example. Meet Sam, a first-time investor. In 2008, as the financial crisis was unfolding, Sam had saved up a considerable amount that she wanted to invest in a mutual fund. However, the market turmoil scared her off, and she decided to hold on to her cash, waiting for a 'better time' to invest. The 'better time,' according to Sam, was when the markets were calm, showing only signs of growth. She ended up waiting, and she waited until 2013, missing out on the significant market recovery that occurred during those years. By the time Sam invested, she had missed out on several years of potential growth, all due to fear.

On the other hand, let's consider Alex, another investor. She also had money to invest in 2008. However, despite the unfolding crisis, Alex chose to invest her money in a mutual fund. Sure, she saw her investment value decrease initially, but she didn't let fear drive her decisions. Alex understood that investing is a long-term game and that market downturns were temporary. Over the next few years, as the market recovered, so did her mutual fund investment. By 2013, not only had she recouped her initial investment, but she also made substantial gains.

The fear of losing money is natural, especially when you're new to investing. However, giving in to this fear can lead to missed opportunities. Stock market investments are about long-term growth, and temporary downturns should not deter your investment journey. When it comes to investing, fear is not your friend.

Sometimes, investing might seem like a leap of faith, but let's break it down together using some hypothetical scenarios that I created with my Investment Inspiration Calculator. While we all have those moments of doubt, the beauty of investing is seeing how small, consistent efforts can lead to surprising outcomes. I've created the perfect tool to do it.

Before we dive into the examples, it's crucial to understand that these are only examples.

They are hypothetical scenarios, and while 10% might be an average rate for mutual fund performance, it's by no means a guarantee. No one can predict the exact future growth, but these examples can give us an idea.

Want to do your own scenarios? Use the QR code below to gain access to the Investment Inspiration Calculator.

Imagine you decide to invest $100 every month. It might not seem like much at first, but with a hypothetical 10% rate of return over 23 years, your total deposits of $27,000 would transform into a whopping $100,000. Extend that effort to 30 years, only seven more years, and from deposits totaling a mere $36,000, you might see a sum of $225,000. It's like nurturing a small plant and watching it grow into a large tree.

If you can set aside $200 monthly, in 23 years, you'd potentially have $200,000. Given the same 30 years, with $72,000 in deposits, it could rise to $450,000. This kind of growth is like a small snowball rolling down a hill, picking up more and more snow until you have a huge boulder-sized mass of wealth.

What about if you aim a little higher by investing $250 each month? In 36 years, you might reach that illustrious $1,000,000 mark. Your total deposits are only $108,000, with the returns doing all the heavy lifting to make up the difference.

With time, patience, and consistency, your contributions could grow far beyond what you might expect. Think of investing and growing your wealth like a long road trip. Sure, there'll be some bumps, maybe even an unexpected detour or two. Along the way, you'll learn, you'll grow, you'll see some significant beauty, and you'll celebrate the small victories.

Why wait? Start today. Even if it's saving $50 a month. Every meaningful journey starts with a single, straightforward step. Investing isn't only about numbers or goals; it's about creating your personal financial story. The examples I've provided are based on general patterns, but the real effort, the heart you put in—that's all you. And when you're ready to take that first step, please share it with me. I am genuinely excited for you and want to celebrate with you. Let's embark on this financial adventure together and uncover what the future holds.

Prompt: Flip back to Chapter 6 and take a look at your Prosperity Blueprint. Your investments should be under the "Savings" category. Now, take a look at "what's left over." Could you add some of "what's left over" to your investments? Play around with the Investment inspiration calculator.

With your current investments, you could possibly see growth to the tune of:

_____ in 23 years

_____ in 30 years

_____ in 36 years

If you added $50 more per month to your investments, you could see:

_____ in 23 years

_____ in 30 years

_____ in 36 years

If you added $150 more per month to your investments, you could see:

_____ in 23 years

_____ in 30 years

_____ in 36 years

Get inspired, and your wealth can grow!

I AM CAPABLE OF

ACHIEVING
FINANCIAL SUCCESS

AND HAPPINESS

IN MY LIFE.

CHAPTER 12

CELEBRATING SUCCESSES

W hile this book is filled with practical strategies, it's essential to acknowledge that the cornerstone of any successful journey lies in your mindset. As I've mentioned before, success is 95% mindset! This is why the celebration of our victories, no matter how big or small, plays such a crucial role.

It's easy to forget to celebrate our wins, especially if we think they are small or commonplace. Whether they're steps towards building a secure financial future, raising our children to be amazing humans, or starting a business from scratch, recognizing and celebrating these accomplishments really helps us develop a positive mindset, fuel our drive, and create momentum that continues to propel us forward.

Recognized publications like the Harvard Business Review, Inc. Magazine, and Forbes have consistently emphasized that celebrating success leads to enduring positive behavior. A recent Harvard Business Review article called "Celebrate to Win" talked about how individuals who reflect on and celebrate their achievements will create more success through increased confidence and motivation. The article discourages the 'onto-the-next' mindset and supports celebrating victories, minor or major, as important parts of personal and professional growth. It describes how celebrations reinforce lessons learned, solidify relationships, and create a sense of achievement while building a foundation for future successes.

In my NeuroCoaching certification program, I learned that celebration isn't only a feel-good factor - it has a profound physiological impact on our brains. When we celebrate, our brain releases dopamine, a neurotransmitter linked to feelings of accomplishment and pleasure. This reinforces the positive behavior, increasing the likelihood of its recurrence, a concept known as positive reinforcement.

Additionally, our brains release more dopamine when we anticipate a reward or celebration, motivating us to take action toward our goals. This cycle of achievement and reward paves the way for continuous progress.

Celebrations also stimulate the release of serotonin, a hormone associated with happiness and well-being. High serotonin levels can lead to increased contentment, happiness, and focus, enhancing our overall life outlook, including our financial journey. Celebrating success also plays a significant role in stress management. It reduces the level of the hormone cortisol, which helps eliminate stress. Lower stress levels foster better decision-making, a critical aspect of financial planning and wealth-building.

And celebrating doesn't always mean spending lots of money! Sometimes, it's the small, thoughtful things that count the most. For instance, when I got my first coaching client, I wanted to celebrate in a special way. There's this lovely store near my house that sells crystals and unique rocks called Bey's Rock Shop. This place isn't just a shop. It's like a miniature wonderland of treasures. Every corner is filled with unique and vibrant stones, from tiny glittering crystals smaller than a marble to massive rocks larger than a basketball. It's a place of discovery, run by a warm, knowledgeable, and friendly family who have spent years collecting these gems from around the world.

For this momentous occasion, I didn't want the usual crystal or bracelet I typically go for when I visit the shop. I wanted something truly special, something that would catch my eye and heart the moment I saw it.

Among the maze of stunning stones, I found an exceptional slice of a rock. Picture this - a thin sliver, less than ¼ inch thick, of ultra-shiny glittering rock. The vibrant hues were framed with a dramatic black border and by a mysterious gray-purple ring circling the heart of the rock. At its center, white crystalline formations sparkled like a snowy oasis.

Smooth to the touch and sparkling under the store light, the slice was about the size of my hand. This piece of wonder was only $10, but in my heart, it was worth so much more. I call it my "first coaching client chip." Every time I look at it, sitting proudly on my desk, I'm filled with a wave of pride and joy. It represents a significant milestone (no pun intended, as it is literally a stone) in my career, one I am proud to have achieved.

Remember, your celebrations don't need to be extravagant or expensive. Their real value lies in the joy you create around them and the personal significance they hold. As you journey towards financial independence, pause to acknowledge and celebrate every step, however small. Each stride you make and each goal you reach is a testament to your progress and determination. That is worth celebrating! I can also personally attest to the electrifying power of celebrating together in a community.

Celebrating our milestones with others who are striving for similar goals can heighten our individual triumphs and multiply the happiness we feel. In my Financially Empowered Sisterhood (FES), we create this energy every time we gather and acknowledge and celebrate a win, big or small. This Sisterhood is open to women who want to be a part of a compassionate community where we create a positive relationship with money and appreciate the importance of acknowledging every stride we make on our wealth-building journey. We celebrate our milestones together and cheer each other on.

In the FES community, we understood that every victory, every step forward, whether big or small, is worth a pause and applause. We believed in not only progressing but also reveling in our shared journey towards financial independence. We noticed that if it's possible for one person, it's possible for everyone, no matter where you are starting. And that is so much easier to see when you are in a group.

Take Louise, for example. A vibrant member from the UK, she began her journey in FES feeling a little overwhelmed, especially when it came to understanding investments. As the sessions rolled on and she gained more knowledge about the subject, something incredible happened. Louise discovered her own financial empowerment. She began to see that she didn't necessarily need a financial advisor to navigate the investment landscape as she originally thought she did before joining the program. With the tools and insights from FES, she began to confidently manage her own finances, adapting US-centric advice to her UK context. By the end of our time together, Louise had not just grown in knowledge but was glowing with confidence, ready to tackle her financial future with pride and enthusiasm.

This is the power of community, of sisterhood. When we're in a group and rally behind each other, each triumph is our own. Every win, every "aha!" moment, is proof that with the right support and tools, we all have what it takes to soar financially. If one member can do it, any of us can. And in FES, we make sure every sister knows that.

We get to feel strong and create positive energy. This energy makes our accomplishments feel even bigger and inspires others to aim for their own wins. When we celebrate together, it's like a domino effect of success and inspiration. Sometimes, the world doesn't recognize how hard we work, especially when it comes to building wealth. But when we celebrate together, we show that our efforts are important, and we're proud of our progress. Our shared progress helps light the way for each of us on our individual journeys.

In this spirit of shared celebration and continuous progress, let's reflect on the wisdom of Bill Gates with one of my favorite quotes: "We overestimate what we can do in one year and underestimate what we can in ten." Achievements and progress often catch us by surprise. When we finally pause to look back, we are often astounded by how far we've come.

I recall a powerful retreat I attended in New Orleans, created by my mentor and writing coach, Sara Connell. One of the exercises she had us engage in was to dive deep into our past, present, and future. As I looked back on where I was five years ago, I was astounded by the huge changes and the significant progress I had made in my business. I had not only met but surpassed my goals. It's an exciting feeling to realize that you're now living a reality that was beyond even your wildest dreams five years ago. This realization helped me to pause and celebrate all of it.

As you navigate your own journey, I encourage you to pause every now and then to appreciate your progress. You've likely come further than you give yourself credit for!

If we can achieve such growth without noticing, what more can we do if we are conscious of a goal and work toward it? As I look to the future, it's time to dream big. I envision a mission for myself: To help one million women build a strong financial future and bring their wealth-creation goals to fruition.

Let's take a moment to appreciate that number: *one million*. One million women with individual dreams and aspirations, using the insights and strategies I've shared to become stronger financially and economically. They'll make smart decisions, invest wisely, and build robust financial foundations for themselves and their families.

Exciting, isn't it? That's the vision I'm passionately pursuing. And I'm sharing it with you so you can be in celebration with me when I finally achieve it. But I am also prepared to be patient and give the journey the time it needs. I'm ready to learn and grow, and I can't wait to celebrate each and every milestone along the way. What will your vision be?

All these celebrations, big or small, fuel our brains. Each celebration nudges us to go beyond our comfort zone, take more risks, grow, and have more faith in ourselves. With each moment of celebration, we motivate ourselves to go the extra mile.

I CAN
SURROUND MYSELF WITH
POSITIVE, SUCCESSFUL,
WEALTHY PEOPLE
WHO INSPIRE ME.

Let's kick off the first celebration right now. You've made it to the end of this book! You've diligently read, absorbed information, and taken significant steps toward financial security. You've created a vision for yourself, a dream, a goal. You've reprogrammed your mindset by removing any prosperity blockers. You created a better relationship with money and have learned to master your money behaviors, too. You have now created your own personal Prosperity Blueprint, optimized your finances, and even learned how to get started in investing in mutual funds. This alone deserves a thoughtful celebration!

Here's what I want you to do now. I want you to tell me how you're celebrating. How are you marking this major milestone in your journey towards creating a path to prosperity? I'm genuinely interested to know and want you to reach out to me personally. I'm collecting all of these celebrations so we can share in this energy together!

Follow this QR code to share inside the book portal:

As you move forward in your journey on your path to prosperity, remember to pause, reflect, and celebrate each step, no matter how small. Every single step is a stride towards your dream. Every step is a victory. And that, my friend, is absolutely worth celebrating.

Take your dreams of prosperity to heart, step forward with confidence, and embark on your wealth-building journey. You're now equipped with the tools and knowledge needed. Step out there and let your light shine! Remember to celebrate the small victories along the way and never lose sight of the fact that building wealth is a marathon, not a sprint. Each day presents a new opportunity for financial growth, and it's the steady, consistent progress that will get you there. The path to prosperity and wealth building is a journey that can seem daunting and scary at first. And that's perfectly okay. Remember, we weren't born knowing how to walk. We learned one step at a time, often with the help of those who had mastered it before us. The same principle applies to creating your path to prosperity.

Partnering with a financial mentor on your journey toward financial independence can have a profound impact. They offer more than technical advice and expertise; they are your cheerleaders and accountability partners, accompanying you on your path to financial success. As a business financial coach myself, I've witnessed the transformative power of such partnerships.

Finding the right mentor means finding someone who will walk the financial journey with you, a companion who will help you navigate every curve and corner with confidence. With the right mentor, you're not only on a path to financial independence - you're on the highway to financial success. Your victories, big or small, become a shared joy that propels you forward.

Also being a part of a community where others are there for you in your moments of triumph, sharing in your victories and encouraging you towards your next goals. The path to prosperity is filled with milestones, both big and small, and who better to share those celebrations with than a group of women who are also on this journey? Their support can inspire and motivate you, turning the financial planning process into an exciting path of personal growth and accomplishment. I've personally made some of my closest friends in online communities and programs that I never would have met otherwise. I am so thankful and grateful for expanding my circle of friends in this way.

Step forward, dream big, and remember you don't have to do it alone. Reach out and find a mentor and community to create the financial future you deserve.

This is the journey of your lifetime. As you step into your financial power, embrace it with anticipation and joy because "the best is truly yet to come!"

Final Prompt: CELEBRATE! You've finished this book and taken the first step to becoming a financial powerhouse. How does it feel? Reflect here:

_____

_____

_____

_____

_____

_____

_____

_____

_____

_____

_____

_____

_____

_____

_____

_____

_____

I AM A
FINANCIAL
POWERHOUSE.

ABOUT THE AUTHOR

A udrey Faust is a financial business coach, mother, wife, and CEO of Audrey Faust Consulting. With over 25 years in finance, she founded her company to help women financially empower themselves and grow their businesses profitably. Audrey holds an accounting degree and an MBA. She is also a certified NeuroCoach, bringing a wealth of knowledge and personal experience to her coaching practice.

www.ingramcontent.com/pod-product-compliance
Lightning Source LLC
Chambersburg PA
CBHW040854210326
41597CB00029B/4843